CHINA NAVAL MODERNIZATION: IMPLICATION FOR U.S. NAVY CAPABILITIES

CHINA NAVAL MODERNIZATION: IMPLICATION FOR U.S. NAVY CAPABILITIES

RONALD O'ROURKE

Nova Science Publishers, Inc.
New York

Copyright © 2008 by Nova Science Publishers, Inc.

All rights reserved. No part of this book may be reproduced, stored in a retrieval system or transmitted in any form or by any means: electronic, electrostatic, magnetic, tape, mechanical photocopying, recording or otherwise without the written permission of the Publisher.

For permission to use material from this book please contact us:
Telephone 631-231-7269; Fax 631-231-8175
Web Site: http://www.novapublishers.com

NOTICE TO THE READER

The Publisher has taken reasonable care in the preparation of this book, but makes no expressed or implied warranty of any kind and assumes no responsibility for any errors or omissions. No liability is assumed for incidental or consequential damages in connection with or arising out of information contained in this book. The Publisher shall not be liable for any special, consequential, or exemplary damages resulting, in whole or in part, from the readers' use of, or reliance upon, this material.

Independent verification should be sought for any data, advice or recommendations contained in this book. In addition, no responsibility is assumed by the publisher for any injury and/or damage to persons or property arising from any methods, products, instructions, ideas or otherwise contained in this publication.

This publication is designed to provide accurate and authoritative information with regard to the subject matter covered herein. It is sold with the clear understanding that the Publisher is not engaged in rendering legal or any other professional services. If legal or any other expert assistance is required, the services of a competent person should be sought. FROM A DECLARATION OF PARTICIPANTS JOINTLY ADOPTED BY A COMMITTEE OF THE AMERICAN BAR ASSOCIATION AND A COMMITTEE OF PUBLISHERS.

LIBRARY OF CONGRESS CATALOGING-IN-PUBLICATION DATA

China naval modernization : implications for U.S. Navy capabilities / Ronald O'Rourke (editor).
   p. cm.
  ISBN 978-1-60456-709-0 (pbk.)
  1. China. Zhongguo ren min jie fang jun. Hai jun--Reorganization. 2. United States. Navy--Reorganization. 3. China--Military policy. 4. Sea-power--China. 5. United States--Military policy. 6. Sea-power--United States. I. O'Rourke, Ronald.
  VA633.C545 2008
  359'.030951--dc22
                    2008018254

Published by Nova Science Publishers, Inc. ✢ New York

CONTENTS

Preface		vii
Chapter 1	Introduction	1
Chapter 2	Background	5
Chapter 3	Potential Oversight Issues for Congress	47
Chapter 4	Legislative Activity for FY2008	69
Appendix	Additional Details on China's Naval Modernization Efforts	71
References		97
Index		125

PREFACE

Concern has grown in Congress and elsewhere about China's military modernization. The topic is an increasing factor in discussions over future required U.S. Navy capabilities. The issue for Congress addressed in this book is: How should China's military modernization be factored into decisions about U.S. Navy programs?

Several elements of China's military modernization have potential implications for future required U.S. Navy capabilities. These include theater-range ballistic missiles (TBMs), land-attack cruise missiles (LACMs), anti-ship cruise missiles (ASCMs), surface-to-air missiles (SAMs), land-based aircraft, submarines, surface combatants, amphibious ships, naval mines, nuclear weapons, and possibly high-power microwave (HPM) devices. China's naval limitations or weaknesses include capabilities for operating in waters more distant from China, joint operations, C4ISR (command, control, communications, computers, intelligence, surveillance, and reconnaissance), long-range surveillance and targeting systems, anti-air warfare (AAW), antisubmarine warfare (ASW), mine countermeasures (MCM), and logistics.

Observers believe a near-term focus of China's military modernization is to field a force that can succeed in a short-duration conflict with Taiwan and act as an anti-access force to deter U.S. intervention or delay the arrival of U.S. forces, particularly naval and air forces, in such a conflict. Some analysts speculate that China may attain (or believe that it has attained) a capable maritime anti-access force, or elements of it, by about 2010. Other observers believe this will happen later. Potential broader or longer-term goals of China's naval modernization include asserting China's regional military leadership and protecting China's maritime territorial, economic, and energy interests.

China's naval modernization has potential implications for required U.S. Navy capabilities in terms of preparing for a conflict in the Taiwan Strait area, maintaining U.S. Navy presence and military influence in the Western Pacific, and countering Chinese ballistic missile submarines. Preparing for a conflict in the Taiwan Strait area could place a premium on the following: on-station or early-arriving Navy forces, capabilities for defeating China's maritime anti-access forces, and capabilities for operating in an environment that could be characterized by information warfare and possibly electromagnetic pulse (EMP) and the use of nuclear weapons.

Certain options are available for improving U.S. Navy capabilities by 2010; additional options, particularly in shipbuilding, can improve U.S. Navy capabilities in subsequent years. China's naval modernization raises potential issues for Congress concerning the role of China in Department of Defense (DOD) and Navy planning; the size of the Navy; the Pacific Fleet's share of the Navy; forward homeporting of Navy ships in the Western Pacific; the number of aircraft carriers, submarines, and ASW-capable platforms; Navy missile defense, air-warfare, AAW, ASW, and mine warfare programs; Navy computer network security; and EMP hardening of Navy systems. This report will be updated as events warrant.

Chapter 1

INTRODUCTION

CONGRESSIONAL AND NAVY CONCERN

Concern has grown in Congress and elsewhere since the 1990s about China's military modernization and its potential implications for required U.S. military capabilities. China's military modernization is an increasing element in discussions of future U.S. Navy requirements. A May 2005 press report, for example, stated that:

> China is one of the central issues, along with terrorism and weapons of mass destruction, in the U.S. military's 2005 Quadrennial Defense Review, a congressionally directed study of military plans.... [W]hen the [then-]chief of naval operations, Adm. Vern Clark, held a classified briefing for congressional defense committees earlier this month about threats, his focus was "mainly" on China, about which he is "gravely concerned," recalled John W. Warner, the Virginia Republican who chairs the Senate Armed Services Committee....
>
> China has come up repeatedly in congressional debate over the size of the Navy. The 288-ship fleet of today is half the size it was three decades ago. "You never want to broadcast to the world that something's insufficient," Warner says, "but clearly China poses a challenge to the sizing of the U.S. Navy."[1]

In an address delivered on February 7, 2007, Secretary of the Navy Donald Winter stated:

> Naval forces must be ready, above all, to conduct major combat operations should the need arise.

We cannot ignore events and trends that reinforce that belief. A recent White Paper prepared by the Chinese military outlined a three-step strategy for modernizing its defense, to include its blue-water ambitions. The third step in their strategy states as a strategic goal "building modernized armed forces and being capable of winning modern, net-centric wars by the mid-21st century." This document implicitly suggests that China hopes to be in a position to successfully challenge the United States, a challenge that would certainly entail blue-water operations.

Public declarations such as this statement and many others serve as reminders that we must be prepared for a world that does not always follow our preferences. Of course, we hope that China will choose a peaceful path. But hope is not a strategy, so we must be prepared.

Those who might be tempted to dismiss or discount the need to be prepared for major combat operations ought to keep in mind that their goodwill and optimism towards totalitarian regimes may not be reciprocated.[2]

A press article reporting on an April 3, 2007, address by Admiral Michael Mullen, the current Chief of Naval Operations, stated that in addition to other topics,

> The admiral also commented on the threats that drive military spending needs. For example, he noted, China is building a new, modernized navy.
>
> "The Chinese are shifting from land-centric" forces as their main focus "to air-centric and naval-centric" buildups. China is acquiring cutting-edge aircraft, new destroyers, four new classes of submarines, and hundreds of radar-guided missiles. "Those investments very much have our attention," Mullen said.[3]

Another short news article, reporting on comments made by Mullen at a breakfast meeting in early May 2007, stated that:

> In response to a question about the need for large Navy vessels, Mullen [told] attendees that while he doesn't expect to see big sea battles, the service has to be mindful of China's naval build up. "China is very actively investing in their navy, building more ships each year. Their building rate is much higher than ours right now," he says. "We have to be mindful of that. Not to be mindful of that would be irresponsible."[4]

Introduction

ISSUE FOR CONGRESS

The issue for Congress addressed in this report is: How should China's military modernization be factored into decisions about U.S. Navy programs? Congress's decisions on this issue could significantly affect future U.S. Navy capabilities, U.S. Navy funding requirements, and the U.S. defense industrial base, including the shipbuilding industry.

SCOPE OF REPORT

This book focuses on the implications that certain elements of China's military modernization may have for future required U.S. Navy capabilities. It does not discuss the following:

- other elements of China's military modernization that may be less relevant to future required U.S. Navy capabilities;
- the potential implications of China's military modernization for parts of DOD other than the Navy (such as the Air Force and the Missile Defense Agency), federal agencies other than DOD (such as the Department of State), and countries other than the United States; and
- China's foreign or economic policy, U.S. defense policy toward Taiwan, or the political likelihood of a military conflict involving China and the United States over Taiwan or some other issue.

TERMINOLOGY

For convenience, this report uses the term China's naval modernization, even though some of the military modernization efforts that could affect required U.S. Navy capabilities are occurring in other parts of China's military, such as the air force or the missile force.

China's military is formally called the People's Liberation Army, or PLA. Its navy is called the PLA Navy, or PLAN, and its air force is called the PLA Air Force, or PLAAF. The PLA Navy includes an air component that is called the PLA Naval Air Force, or PLANAF. China refers to its ballistic missile force as the Second Artillery Force.

SOURCES

Sources of information for this book, all of which are unclassified, include the following:

- the 2007 edition DOD's annual report to Congress on China's military power, which was released on May 25, 2007, and previous annual editions of this report;[5]
- the 2004 edition of *Worldwide Maritime Challenges*, a publication of the U.S. Navy's Office of Naval Intelligence (ONI);[6]
- China's 2006 and 2004 defense white papers;[7]
- the prepared statements and transcript of a July 27, 2005, hearing on China grand strategy and military modernization before the House Armed Services Committee;[8]
- the prepared statements for March 16, 2006, and September 15, 2005, hearings on China's military modernization before the U.S.-China Economic and Security Review Commission, an advisory body created by the FY2001 defense authorization act (P.L. 106398) and subsequent legislation,[9] and the prepared statements and published transcript of a similar hearing before the commission on February 6, 2004;[10]
- a 2007 report on China's military antiaccess strategies and a 2005 report on China's defense industry, both by the RAND Corporation;[11]
- a 2003 report on China's military power by an independent task force sponsored by the Council on Foreign Relations;[12]
- open-source military reference sources such as the Jane's Information Group; and
- journal articles and news articles, including articles from the defense trade press.[13]

Chapter 2

BACKGROUND

CHINA'S NAVAL MODERNIZATION

Maritime-Relevant Elements of China's Military Modernization [14]

This section summarizes elements of China's military modernization that may have implications for required U.S. Navy capabilities. See Appendix A for additional details and commentary on several of these modernization activities.

Theater-Range Ballistic Missiles (TBMs)

One of the most prominent elements of China's military modernization has been the deployment of large numbers of theater-range ballistic missiles (TBMs)[15] capable of attacking targets in Taiwan or other regional locations. Among these are CSS-6 and CSS-7 short-range ballistic missiles (SRBMs) deployed in locations across from Taiwan. DOD states that China as of October 2006 had deployed 875 to 975 CSS-6 and CSS-7 TBMs, and that this total is increasing at a rate of more than 100 missiles per year.[16]

Although ballistic missiles in the past have traditionally been used to attack fixed targets on land, DOD and other observers believe China is developing TBMs equipped with maneuverable reentry vehicles (MaRVs) capable of hitting moving ships at sea. In January 2007, the Director of National Intelligence stated:

> The Chinese are developing more capable long-range conventional strike systems and short- and medium-range ballistic missiles with terminally guided maneuverable warheads able to attack US carriers and airbases.[17]

Observers have expressed strong concern about this development, because such missiles, in combination with broad-area maritime surveillance and targeting systems, would permit China to attack moving U.S. Navy ships in the Western Pacific. The U.S. Navy has not previously faced a threat from highly accurate ballistic missiles capable of hitting moving ships at sea. Due to their ability to change course, MaRVs would be more difficult to intercept than non-maneuvering ballistic missile reentry vehicles. DOD states that:

> To prevent deployment of naval forces into western Pacific waters, PLA planners are focused on targeting surface ships at long ranges. Analyses of current and projected force structure improvements suggest that in the near term, China is seeking the capacity to hold surface ships at risk through a layered defense that reaches out to the "second island chain" (i.e., the islands extending south and east from Japan, to and beyond Guam in the western Pacific Ocean). One area of apparent investment emphasis involves a combination of medium-range ballistic missiles, C4ISR for geo-location of targets, and onboard guidance systems for terminal homing to strike surface ships on the high seas or their onshore support infrastructure. This capability would have particular significance, owing to the preemptive and coercive options it would provide China in a regional crisis.[18]

According to a 2005 press report, "navy officials project [that such missiles] could be capable of targeting US warships from sometime around 2015."[19]

Land-Attack Cruise Missiles (LACMs)

China is developing land-attack cruise missiles (LACMs) that can be fired from land bases, land-based aircraft, or Navy platforms such as submarines to attack targets, including air and naval bases, in Taiwan or other regional locations, such as Japan or Guam. DOD states that "First- and second-generation LACMs may be deployed in the near future."[20] The U.S. Defense Intelligence Agency (DIA) stated in 2005 that "We judge that by 2015, [China] will have hundreds of highly accurate air- and ground-launched LACMs."[21]

Anti-Ship Cruise Missiles (ASCMs)

China is modernizing its extensive inventory of anti-ship cruise missiles (ASCMs), which can be launched from land-based strike fighters and bombers, surface combatants, submarines and possibly shore-based launchers. Among the most capable of the new ASCMs that have been or are being acquired by the PLA Navy are the Russian-made SS-N-22 Sunburn (carried by China's four Russian-made Sovremenny-class destroyers) and the SS-N.

Current and Projected National Security Threats to the United States, Vice Admiral Lowell E. Jacoby, U.S. Navy, Director, Defense Intelligence Agency, Statement for the Record [before the] Senate Select Committee on Intelligence, 16 February 2005, p. 13. See also Current and Projected National Security Threats to the United States, Vice Admiral Lowell E. Jacoby, U.S. Navy, Director, Defense Intelligence Agency, Statement For the Record [before the] Senate Armed Services Committee, 17 March 2005, p. 13. 27 Sizzler (carried by eight of China's Russian-made Kilo-class submarines). DOD states that "The pace of [China's] indigenous ASCM research, development and production — and of foreign procurement — has accelerated over the past decade."[22]

Surface-to-Air Missiles (SAMs)

China is deploying modern surface-to-air missile (SAM) systems across from Taiwan, including long-range and high-altitude systems that have an advertised range sufficient to cover the entire Taiwan Strait, which is roughly 100 nautical miles (185 kilometers) wide. Advanced SAMs may have some effectiveness against stealthy aircraft. Longer- and shorter- range SAM systems deployed along China's coast opposite Taiwan would in combination give China a multilayer defense against enemy aircraft seeking to operate over the Strait or approach that portion of China's coast.[23]

Land-Based Aircraft

China is introducing increasing numbers of modern and capable (so-called fourth-generation) fighters and strike fighters into the PLA Air Force and PLA Naval Air Force. These include Russian-made Su-27s and Su-30s and indigenously produced FB-7s, F-10s, and F-11s. At least some of the strike fighters will be armed with modern ASCMs. China is also upgrading the ASCMs carried by its land-based maritime bombers. The effectiveness of China's combat aircraft could be enhanced by new support aircraft, including tankers and airborne warning and control system (AWACS) aircraft.

Unmanned Aerial Vehicles (UAVs)

DOD states that "acquisition of UAVs and UCAVs,[24] including the Israeli HARPY [UCAV], expands China's options for long-range reconnaissance and strike."[25]

Submarines

China's submarine modernization effort has attracted substantial attention and concern.[26] The effort in recent years has involved the acquisition of at least five classes of submarines, making it, in terms of number of designs involved, one of the more ambitious submarine-acquisition efforts on record by any country. China by the end of 2006 completed taking delivery on eight Russian-made Kilo-class non-nuclear-powered attack submarines (SSs) that are in addition to four Kilos that China purchased from Russia in the 1990s,[27] and is building four other classes of submarines, including the following:

- a new nuclear-powered ballistic missile submarine (SSBN) design called the Jin class or Type 094;
- a new nuclear powered attack submarine (SSN) design called the Shang class or Type 093;
- a new SS design called the Yuan class or Type 041; and
- another (and also fairly new) SS design called the Song class or Type 039/039G.

These five classes of submarines are expected to be much more modern and capable than China's aging older-generation submarines.

As shown in table 1, China commissioned one to three new submarines per year between 1995 and 2004. Eight new submarines (including five Kilos) were commissioned in 2005, and seven new submarines (including three Kilos) were commissioned in 2006.[28]

PLA Navy submarines are armed with one or more of the following: ASCMs, wire-guided and wake-homing torpedoes, and mines. China's eight recently delivered Kilos are reportedly armed with the highly capable SS-N-27 Sizzler ASCM.[29] China's four older Kilos reportedly are to be refitted in Russia, with the upgrades likely to include the installation of the SS-N-27.

Although ASCMs are often highlighted as sources of concern, wake-homing torpedoes can also be very difficult for surface ships to counter. In addition to some combination of ASCMs, torpedoes, and mines, Jin-class SSBNs will carry a new type of submarine-launched ballistic missile (SLBM), and Shang-class SSNs may carry LACMs.

China's submarine modernization effort is producing a substantially more modern and capable submarine force. As shown in table 1, observers expect China to have a total of 28 Shang, Kilo, Yuan, and Song class submarines in commission by the end of 2007.

Table 1. PLA Navy Submarine Commissionings Actual (1995-2004) and Projected (2005-2010)

	Jin (Type 094) SSBN	Shang (Type 093) SSN	Kilo SS (Russianmade)	Yuan (Type 041) SS	Song (Type 039) SS	Ming (Type 035) SSa	Total
1995			2b			1	3
1996						1	1
1997						2	2
1998			1b			2	3
1999			1b		1		2
2000						1	1
2001					2	1	3
2002						1	1
2003					2		2
2004					3		3
2005			5		3		8
2006		1	3	1	2c		7
2007		1d			n/a		$1
2008	1	n/a		1	n/a		$2
2009		n/a		n/a	n/a		n/a
2010	1e	n/a		n/a	n/a		n/a

Source: *Jane's Fighting Ships 2006-2007*, and previous editions.

a. Figures for Ming-class boats are when the boats were launched (i.e., put into the water for final construction). Actual commissioning dates for these boats may have been later.
b. First four boats, commissioned in the 1990s, are to be refitted in Russia; upgrades are likely to include installation of SS-N-27 ASCM.
c. Unclear whether there will be any additional boats beyond the 12th and 13th shown for 2006.
d. Construction of a third ship may have started but has not been confirmed. A total of 5 boats is expected.
e. Additional units are expected, perhaps at two-year intervals. A total of 4 to 6 boats is expected. One news article, citing information from the Office of Naval Intelligence, states that a total of 5 are expected. (Bill Gertz, "China Expands Sub Fleet," *Washington Times*, March 2, 2007.)

n/a = data not available.

Although China's aging Ming- and Romeo-class submarines are based on old technology and are much less capable than the PLA Navy's newer-design submarines, China may decide that these older boats have continued value as minelayers or as bait or decoy submarines that can be used to draw out enemy submarines (such as U.S. SSNs) that can then be attacked by more modern PLA Navy submarines.[30]

ONI states that "Chinese diesel submarine force levels are stabilizing as quality replaces quantity," and has published a graph accompanying this statement suggesting that the figure may stabilize at a level between 25 and 50.[31]

Another set of observers states:

> In order to grasp the energy that China is now committing to undersea warfare, consider that during 2002-2004 China's navy launched thirteen submarines while simultaneously undertaking the purchase of submarines from Russia on an unprecedented scale. Indeed, China commissioned thirty-one new submarines between 1995 and 2005. Given this rapid evolution, appraisals of China's capability to field competent and lethal diesel submarines in the littorals have slowly changed from ridicule to grudging respect of late. China's potential for complex technological development is fi nally being taken seriously abroad.[32]

Another observer states:

> China's submarine fleet is now considered the PLAN's most "potent strength." Since 1995, the PLAN has commissioned about 31 new submarines, including two nuclear-powered submarines based on advanced Russian technology. Eight submarines were commissioned in 2005, and seven were commissioned in 2006, including new Song-class boats and a Yuan-class boat heavily inspired by Russia's Amur-class sub with its anechoic tile coatings and quiet seven-bladed skewed propeller. The reported incorporation of "air-independent propulsion" systems that permit submarines to operate underwater for up to 30 days would make the Song and Yuan submarines virtually undetectable to existing U.S. surveillance networks.
>
> In addition, China has three new nuclear-powered submarine design and construction programs. The Type-093 Shang-class nuclear attack boat and the Type-094 Jin-class nuclear ballistic missile submarine programs are underway. Two Shang submarines are deployed, and three are under construction, and five older and less sophisticated submarines will likely be employed to screen the higher-value assets. Chinese sources openly describe using certain submarines as "bait." Employing this tactic, it is conceivable that United States submarines could reveal their own presence to lurking Kilos by executing attacks against

nuisance Mings and Romeos. No wonder China continues to operate the vessels, which are widely derided as obsolete by Western observers. The threat from these older submarines cannot be dismissed out of hand. Informal United States Navy testimony suggests that the PLAN can operate the older classes of diesel submarines with surprising tactical efficiency. (Statement of Lyle J. Goldstein and William Murray as printed in *2/6/04 USCC hearing*, p. 153)

Jin-class ballistic missile submarines are reportedly under construction. Five Type-095 submarines, a larger version of the Shang/Jin hull, are also under development.60 Together with its procurement program for improved Russian-made Kilo-class submarines, China has at least six new submarine programs under way simultaneously — a submarine development campaign that is unprecedented in peacetime. China will have at least 34 advanced submarines deployed in the Pacific by 2010 — some analysts expect as many as 50 to 60 — assuming that those under construction will be completed within three years. China will certainly have over 60 advanced submarines by 2020.[33]

Another observer states:

Although China is modernizing its submarine force, it is not "expanding" it. Since the mid-1980s, the force has been in steady decline from nearly 120 boats to roughly 55 operational submarines today. The U.S. Navy expects the force will level out around 40 boats in the next decade.

The decline of the submarine fleet is part of a transition where large older classes are being phased out and replaced with newer but less numerous submarine classes.[34]

Although China is modernizing its submarine force through the construction of new boats, one report, citing U.S. Navy data, shows the annual rate of Chinese submarine patrols to be relatively low. As shown in table 2, over the last five years, according to this report, China's submarine force has conducted an average total of 2.4 individual submarine patrols per year.

The Federation of American Scientists (FAS), which published the figures shown in Table 2, states:

China's entire submarine fleet conducted only two patrols in 2006, according to information declassified by the U.S. Navy and obtained by the Federation of American Scientists under the Freedom of Information Act. The low patrol rate follows a drop from an all-time high of only six patrols in 2000 to none in 2005. China's single sea-launched ballistic missile submarine Xia, the data shows, has never conducted a deterrent patrol.

Table 2. Chinese Submarine Patrols Per Year, 1981-2006

81	82	83	84	85	86	87	88	89	90	91	92	93
1	0	2	2	2	1	1	5	2	0	1	1	0
94	95	96	97	98	99	00	01	02	03	04	05	06
1	1	1	2	3	2	6	3	4	3	3	0	2

Source: Federation of American Scientists (FAS), "China's Submarine Fleet Continues Low Patrol Rate," published online at [http://fas.org/blog/ssp/2007/02/]. FAS states in the online article that it received the data from the U.S. Navy under the Freedom of Information Act (FOIA).

The low level of Chinese submarine patrols is a curious contrast to warnings by the Pentagon, some private institutes and news media that China is expanding its submarine operations deeper into the Pacific. Although Chinese submarines occasionally venture into the waters around Japan and Taiwan, the fleet is surprisingly inactive.

Since 1981, the first year for which patrol data is available, the Chinese submarine force has conducted an average of less than two patrols per year. The highest number of annual patrols conducted since 1981 was six patrols in 2000. In four years (1982, 1990, 1993 and 2005), no patrols were conducted at all. Over the 25-year period, the trend is that patrols have only increased from one per year to approximately 2.8 patrols per year.

If one assumes that U.S. Naval Intelligence's use of the term "patrol" follows the DOD's definitions, then the declassified patrol data suggests that Chinese general purpose submarines in 2006 twice conducted investigations to detect other submarines, participated in naval defense operations in coastal or outside coastal areas, or deployed for the purpose of gathering information or harassing. That implies an almost dormant submarine fleet.

One of the two patrols conducted in 2006 appears to have been the widely reported surfacing of a Song-class diesel-electric submarine near the U.S. aircraft carrier USS Kitty Hawk in the South China Sea. The news media and pundits dramatized the incident as an example of China expanding its submarine operations, the Chinese government downplayed the reports as inaccurate, and the Pentagon said the media made too much of the incident.

The new [Chinese] submarines are more capable than the ones they replace, but the modernization has not resulted in an increase in the number of submarine patrols. On the contrary, during the period between 2000 and 2006, when China acquired a dozen new Kilo and Song class submarines, the number of patrols declined from six to two (with no patrols at all in 2005).

The implications of the low patrol rate are significant. The total operational experience for the entire Chinese submarine force is only 49 patrols in 25 years, corresponding to each submarine conducting an average of one patrol every third year.

As a result, Chinese submarine crews appear to have relatively little operational experience and consequently limited skills in operating their boats safely and competently. It suggests that the tactical skills that would be needed for the Chinese submarine force to operate effectively in a war may be limited.

China continues — at least for now — to use its submarine force as a coastal defense force.[35]

Another observer, expressing a different view on the issue of the frequency of Chinese submarine patrols, states that "Chinese submarines slip out into open seas from underwater tunnels and are virtuallyundetectable." Regarding an October 2006 incident involving a Song-class SS that surfaced near the U.S. aircraft carrier Kitty Hawk while it was operating near Okinawa, this observer states that after the submarine was detected on the surface, the submarine "submerged and disappeared, defeating all U.S. anti-submarine warfare (ASW) efforts to detect it." The observer states that

> The ease with which the submarine maneuvered undetected into Japanese waters and evaded U.S. and Japan Self Defense Force submarine sensors suggests that China's large submarine fleet engages in far more sea patrols than the U.S. has any hope of tracking.[36]

Aircraft Carriers

The issue of whether and when China might deploy one or more aircraft carriers, and what the design and capabilities of Chinese aircraft carriers might be, has been a topic of discussion among government and nongovernment observers for the last several years. DOD states that:

> In October 2006, Lieutenant General Wang Zhiyuan, vice chairman of the Science and Technology Commission of the PLA's General Armament Department stated that the "Chinese army will study how to manufacture aircraft carriers so that we can develop our own .... [A]ircraft carriers are indispensable if we want to protect our interests in oceans."

China first began to discuss developing an indigenous aircraft carrier in the late 1970s. In 1985, China purchased the Australian carrier the HMAS Melbourne. Although the hull was scrapped, Chinese technicians studied the ship and built a replica of its flight deck for pilot training. China purchased two former Soviet carriers — the Minsk in 1998 and the Kiev in 2000. Neither carrier was made operational; instead, they were used as floating military theme parks. Nevertheless, both provided design information to PLA Navy engineers.

In 1998 China purchased the ex-Varyag, a Kuznetsov-class Soviet carrier that was only 70 percent complete at the time of the Soviet Union's collapse. Recent deck refurbishment, electrical work, fresh hull paint with PLA Navy markings, and expressed interest in Russia's Su-33 fighter has re-kindled debate about a Chinese carrier fleet. The PLA's ultimate intentions for the Varyag remain unclear, but a number of possibilities exist: turning it into an operational aircraft carrier, a training or transitional platform, or a floating theme park — its originally-stated purpose.

Regardless of Beijing's final objective for the ex-Varyag, PLA Navy study of the ship's structural design could eventually assist China in creating its own carrier program. Lieutenant General Wang stated that, "we cannot establish a real naval force of aircraft carriers within three or five years." Some analysts in and out of government predict that China could have an operational carrier by the end of the 12th Five-Year Plan (2011-2015); others assess the earliest it could deploy an operational aircraft carrier is 2020 or beyond.[37]

The question of China's potential development and acquisition of aircraft carriers is discussed at length in an article in the Autumn 2006 issue of the *Naval War College Review*.[38]

Surface Combatants

China since the early 1990s has purchased four Sovremenny-class destroyers from Russia and deployed eight new classes of indigenously built destroyers and frigates that demonstrate a significant modernization of PLA Navy surface combatant technology. The introduction of eight new destroyer and frigate designs over a period of about 15 years is an undertaking with few parallels by any country in recent decades. China has also deployed a new kind of fast attack craft that uses a stealthy catamaran hull design.

Sovremenny-Class Destroyers

China in 1996 ordered two Sovremennyclass destroyers from Russia; the ships entered service in 1999 and 2001. China in 2002 ordered two additional Sovremenny-class destroyers from Russia; the ships entered service in 2005 and 2006. Sovremenny-class destroyers are equipped with the SS-N-22 Sunburn ASCM, another highly capable ASCM.[39] DOD says the two ships ordered in 2002 "are fitted with anti-ship cruise missiles (ASCMs) and wide-area air defense systems that feature qualitative improvements over the [two] earlier

SOVREMENNYY-class DDGs China purchased from Russia.[40] China reportedly has an option for another two Sovremenny-class ships.

Five New Indigenously Built Destroyer Classes

China since the early 1990s has built five new classes of destroyers. Compared to China's 16 older Luda (Type 051) class destroyers, which entered service between 1971 and 1991, these 5 new destroyer classes are substantially more modern in terms of their hull designs, propulsion systems, sensors, weapons, and electronics. A key area of improvement in the new destroyer designs is their anti-air warfare (AAW) technology,[41] which has been a significant PLA Navy shortcoming. Like the older Luda-class destroyers, these new destroyer classes are armed with ASCMs.

As shown in table 3, China to date has commissioned only 1 or 2 ships in each of these five classes, suggesting that a key purpose of at least some of these classes may have been to serve as stepping stones in a plan to modernize the PLA Navy's surface combatant technology incrementally before committing to larger-scale series production.[42] If one or more of these designs are put into larger-scale production, it would accelerate the modernization of China's surface combatant force.

The Luhu-class ships reportedly were ordered in 1985 but had their construction delayed by a decision to give priority to the construction of six frigates that were ordered by Thailand. The Luhai-class ship is believed to have served as the basis for the Luyang-class designs. Compared to the Luhai, the Luyang I-class ships appear stealthier. DOD states that the Luyang I design is equipped with the Russian-made SA-N-7B Grizzly SAM and the Chinese-made YJ-83 ASCM.[43]

Table 3. New PLA Navy Destroyer Classes

Class name	Type	Number built	Hull number(s)	In service (actual or projected)
Luhu	052	2	112, 113	1994, 1996
Luhai	051B	1	167	1999
Luyang I	052B	2	168, 169	2004
Luyang II	052C	2	170, 171	2004, 2005
Luzhou	051C	2	115, 116	2006, 2007

Source: Jane's Fighting Ships 2006-2007.

Table 4. New PLA Navy Frigate Classes

Class name	Type	Number built or building	Hull number(s)	In service (actual or projected)
Jiangwei I	053G H2G	4	539-542	1991-1994
Jiangwei II	053H3	10	between 521 and 567	1998-2005
Jiangkai	054	2	525, 526	2005

Source: Jane's Fighting Ships 2006-2007.

The Luyang II-class ships appear to feature an even more capable AAW system that includes a Chinese-made SAM system called the HHQ-9 that has an even longer range, a vertical launch system (VLS), and a phased-array radar that is outwardly somewhat similar to the SPY-1 radar used in the U.S.-made Aegis combat system. Indeed, the Luyang II-class design bears some resemblance to U.S. and Japanese Aegis destroyers, though they are probably not as modern or capable in some respects as the U.S. and Japanese ships.[44]

DOD says the Luzhou-class design "is designed for anti-air warfare. It will be equipped with the Russian SA-N-20 SAM system controlled by the TOMBSTONE phased-array radar. The SA-N-20 more than doubles the range of current PLA Navy air defense systems marking a significant improvement in China's ship-borne air defense capability."[45]

Three New Indigenously Built Frigate Classes

China since the early 1990s has built three new classes of frigates that are more modern than China's 31 older Jianghu (Type 053) class frigates, which entered service between the mid-1970s and 1989. The three new frigate classes, like the new destroyer classes, feature improved AAW capabilities. Unlike the new destroyer designs, at least two of the new frigate designs have been put into larger-scale series production. Table 4 summarizes the three new classes.

Construction of Jiangwei I-class ships appears to have ceased. It is unclear whether construction of Jiangwei II-class ships will continue after the 10th ship. A third Jiangkai-class ship may be under construction, but this has not yet been confirmed.[46] The Jiangkai-class ships feature a stealthy design that somewhat resembles France's La Fayette-class frigate, which first entered service in 1996.[47]

Houbei-Class Fast Attack Craft. In addition to its 190 older fast attack craft (including 37 armed with ASCMs), China in 2004 introduced a new type of ASCM-armed fast attack craft, called the Houbei class, that uses a stealthy, wave-piercing, catamaran hull. Observers believe the hull design — one of the more advanced used by any navy in the world today — is based on a design developed by a firm in Australia, a country which is a world leader in high-speed catamaran designs. At least four of these new fast attack craft are now in service. A large number additional units are expected as replacements for China's older and less-advanced fast attack craft, although one observer states that production of the Houbei-class design has not been as fast as originally expected."[48]

Amphibious Ships

China since 2003 has built three new classes of amphibious ships and landing craft. Each type has been built at three or four shipyards. Between these three classes, China built a total of 19 amphibious ships and 10 amphibious landing craft in 2003-2005.

Mine Countermeasures (MCM) Ships

China is building a new class of mine countermeasures (MCM) ship, called the Wozang class. The first unit was commissioned in 2005, and a total of 10 to 15 are expected. One observer states that the Wozang-class design "looks remarkably similar to the 1950s vintage T43 class," and that "further units have failed to materialise so far, although mine-countermeasures is perhaps the weakest part of the Chinese naval inventory."[49]

Naval Mines

Regarding naval mines, ONI states:

> China is developing and exporting numerous advanced mines of all types. One example is the wireless remote controlled EM57, a mine that offers many tactical options. For example, the mine can be turned off and on remotely to prolong its life, or it can be activated and deactivated to allow safe passage for friendly vessels.[50]

> DOD stated in 2003 that the PLA's mines include bottom and moored influence mines, mobile mines, remotely controlled mines, command-detonated mines, and propelled-warhead mines. Use of propelled-warhead mines in deep waters has the potential to deny enemy naval formations large operational areas.[51]

DOD stated in 2002 that China "likely has enough mine warfare assets to lay a good defensive and a modest offensive minefield using a wide variety of launch platforms."[52]

Another observer stated in a presentation that China has

a large inventory of mines. And we see a tremendous interest in some of the most modern deadly mines going. These deep water rising mines [on the projection screen] can be purchased from Russia. They have tremendous ability to mine deeper waters where we would prefer to operate. So what we would consider to have been a haven [for U.S. Navy ships] may no longer be a haven.[53]

Information Warfare/Information Operations (IW/IO)

China open-source writings demonstrate an interest in information warfare (IW), also called information operations (IO), as an increasingly important element of warfare, particularly against a sophisticated opposingforce such as the U.S. military. Concern about potential PLA IW/IO capabilities has been heightened by recent press reports about attacks on U.S. computer systems that in some cases appear to have originated in China.[54] One observer has stated that "China even now is planting viruses in U.S. computer systems that they will activate" in the event of a military conflict with the United States.[55] DOD states that

> There has been much writing on information warfare among China's military thinkers, who indicate a strong conceptual understanding of its methods and uses....
>
> The PLA is investing in electronic countermeasures, defenses against electronic attack (e.g., electronic and infrared decoys, angle reflectors, and false target generators), and computer network operations (CNO). China's CNO concepts include computer network attack, computer network defense, and computer network exploitation. The PLA sees CNO as critical to achieving "electromagnetic dominance" early in a conflict. Although there is no evidence of a formal Chinese CNO doctrine, PLA theorists have coined the term "Integrated Network Electronic Warfare" to prescribe the use of electronic warfare, CNO, and kinetic strikes to disrupt battlefield network information systems.
>
> The PLA has established information warfare units to develop viruses to attack enemy computer systems and networks, and tactics and measures to protect friendly computer systems and networks. In 2005, the PLA began to incorporate offensive CNO into its exercises, primarily in first strikes against enemy networks.[56]
>
> In January 2007, the Director of the Defense Intelligence Agency stated:
>
> China has developed an apparent large scale CNO [computer network operations] program, including military exercises to refine and implement concepts. China's robust presence in the global IT [information technology] hardware and software supply chain enhances its technical expertise and IO capability. China is the number one IT hardware provider for U.S. consumers,

accounting for 42 percent of U.S. IT hardware imports in 2005. As such, U.S. dependence on China for certain items critical to the U.S. defense industry and the waning of U.S. global IT dominance are valid concerns that demand vigilance.[57]

Nuclear Weapons[58]

China, as a longstanding nuclear weapon state, could put nuclear warheads on weapons such as TBMs, LACMs, ASCMs, torpedoes, and naval mines. China could use nuclear-armed versions of these weapons (except the LACMs) to attack U.S. Navy ships at sea. China might do so in the belief that it could subsequently confuse the issue in the public arena of whose nuclear warhead had detonated,[59] or that the United States in any event would not escalate the conflict by retaliating with a nuclear attack on a land target in China. During the Cold War, analysts debated whether the use of a Soviet nuclear weapon against U.S. Navy ships during a conflict would lead to a U.S. nuclear response.

China could also use a nuclear-armed ballistic missile to detonate a nuclear warhead in the atmosphere to create a high-altitude electromagnetic pulse (EMP) intended to temporarily or permanently disable the electronic circuits of U.S. or other civilian and military electronic systems. Some observers have expressed concern in recent years over the potential vulnerability of U.S. military systems to EMP effects.[60]

High-Power Microwave (HPM) Weapons

Some observers are concerned that China might develop or already possess high-power microwave (HPM) weapons, also called radio frequency weapons (RFWs) or E-bombs, which are non-nuclear devices that can be used to generate damaging EMP effects over relatively short distances to disable the electronic circuits of nearby enemy civilian and military systems.[61] In theory, an HPM weapon could be placed on a TBM or ASCM and fired at a U.S. Navy ship. Although the effective EMP radius of such devices might be on the order of only a few hundred yards,[62] such devices could be used to attack individual U.S. Navy ships without the political or escalatory risks of a high-altitude nuclear detonation.[63]

Military Doctrine, Education, Training, Exercises, and Logistics

Military capability is a product not simply of having weapons, but of having a doctrine for how to use them, well-educated and well-trained personnel, realistic exercises, and logistic support. In past years, the PLA was considered weak in some or all of these areas, and PLA military capability consequently was considered not as great as its inventory of weapons alone might suggest. The 2004 China defense white paper states an intention to improve in these areas,[64] and observers believe the PLA is acting on these intentions. DOD stated in 2005 that "China has stated its intentions and allocated resources to pursue force-wide professionalization, improve training, conduct more robust, realistic joint exercises, and accelerate acquisition of modern weapons."[65] DOD stated in 2007 that "In June 2006, the PLA released new guidance to increase realism in training and to expand the use of simulators and opposing forces in training evolutions."[66]

The PLA in recent years has developed a doctrine for joint operations involving multiple military services,[67] improved its military education and training and conducted more realistic exercises,[68] and reformed its logistics system.[69] Improvements in these areas might be considered as important as the weapon-modernization activities discussed above. Some of these improvements may require several years to fully implement.

China's Naval Limitations and Weaknesses

In spite of the concerns raised by the modernization effort described above, observers believe PLA military (including naval) forces continue to have limitations or weaknesses in the following areas, among others:

- sustained operations in waters and air space that are more distant from China;
- joint operations;
- C4ISR (command, control, communications, computers, intelligence, surveillance and reconnaissance) systems, including, for example, airborne warning and control system (AWACS) capabilities;
- long-range surveillance and targeting systems for detecting and tracking ships at sea — a capability needed to take full advantage of longer-ranged anti-ship weapons;
- anti-air warfare (AAW) capability for defending surface ships against air attack;
- antisubmarine warfare (ASW) capability for defending surface ships against submarine attack;
- mine countermeasures (MCM) capability; and
- logistics.

The paragraphs below elaborate on these items.

Weaknesses and Limitations in General

Regarding weaknesses and limitations of China's military in general, a 2007 report by a task force sponsored by the Council on Foreign Relations stated that despite advances, the PLA confronts many obstacles:

- The sophistication of new equipment generally exceeds current joint command-and-control capabilities.
- Its reliance on a blend of obsolete and modern equipment makes effective large-scale planning, training, and operations difficult.
- Its dependence on multiple foreign arms suppliers makes it hard to build efficient supply chains and maintenance regimes.
- It has a shortage of technically knowledgeable, innovative, initiative-taking personnel who can operate high-tech systems, a deficiency exacerbated by China's lack of a professional corps of noncommissioned officers.
- It has little combat experience — Chinese military forces have not been involved in major combat since 1979, when they performed poorly against Vietnamese forces.
- It lacks many of the instruments of force projection, including long-range bombers, aircraft carriers, large airborne units, and the logistics capability to support and sustain combat forces beyond its borders.

None of these obstacles can be overcome swiftly, and none can be overcome merely by throwing more money at the problem.[70]

Regarding PLA Navy limitations and weaknesses in general, DIA states:

> China continues to develop or import modern weapons.... The PLA must overcome significant integration challenges to turn these new, advanced and disparate weapon systems into improved capabilities. Beijing also faces technical and operational difficulties in numerous areas.[71]

Another set of observers states:

> The PLAN is limited by a lack of integration in its command, control, and communication systems; targeting; air defense; and antisubmarine warfare capabilities. PLAN ships are vulnerable to attack by aircraft, torpedoes, and antiship missiles. The navies of the ASEAN nations could, if able to operate together, exclude the PLAN from the South China Sea....

New capabilities are limited by the lack of some critical supporting systems. The PLAN is deficient in antisubmarine warfare capabilities. PLAN ships are also vulnerable to air attack by both aircraft and antiship missiles.[72]

A separate set of observers states that weaknesses in China's shipbuilding industry

> are more problematic for naval projects [than for commercial shipbuilding projects]. Although China is designing and building increasingly sophisticated warships, Chinese naval shipbuilders still need to import key components or modules, such as propulsion systems, navigation and sensor suites, and major weapon systems, to outfit these vessels. Such a reliance on imported subsystems creates systems-integration challenges, as well as security concerns stemming from dependence on foreign suppliers. China appears to be improving its ability to absorb imported equipment and technologies, but it will take time before these and other problems are overcome.[73]

These observers also state that

> the capabilities of most of China's current naval SAM and SSM systems and much of its naval electronics are limited and not equivalent to U.S. capabilities or those of other Asian militaries. The limited range and accuracy of Chinese SSMs and SAMs create serious problems for air-defense and antisubmarine warfare. Many of these systems also do not operate with over-the-horizon targeting, further degrading their already-limited capabilities.

Furthermore, few — if any — advances were made in the development and production of naval propulsion or navigation equipment in the 1980s or 1990s. This lack continues to be a major weakness in China's domestic naval production efforts, and one that the PLAN's heavy reliance on foreign subsystems for its second-generation vessels testifies to.[74]

Regarding the submarine force, one observer states that

> by no means should the PLAN submarine force be considered ten feet tall. China's submarine force has some significant weaknesses: a reliance on diesel submarines that have to approach the surface to snorkel; especially in the wake of the Ming 361 accident,[75] it is evident that crew training and professionalism remain a fundamental problem; finally, there is little evidence of a robust, remote cueing capability, and probable weakness in the sphere of command and control.[76]

Sustained Operations in Distant Waters

Regarding sustained operations in more distant waters, DOD states: "China's ability to sustain military power at a distance, at present, remains limited...."[77] DOD stated in 2005 that:

> China does not appear to have broadened its concept of operations for anti-access and sea denial to encompass sea control in waters beyond Taiwan and its immediate periphery. If China were to shift to a broader "sea control" strategy, the primary indicators would include: development of an aircraft carrier, development of robust anti-submarine warfare capabilities, development of a true area anti-air warfare capability, acquisition of large numbers of nuclear attack submarines, development of effective maritime C4ISR, and increased open water training....
>
> With its present force structure, according to the Intelligence Community, Chinese surface combatants would have difficulty projecting power into the Strait of Malacca, especially if it were conducting simultaneous blockade or invasion operations elsewhere. Similarly, although the PLA Navy occasionally patrols as far as the Spratly Islands, its limited organic air defense capability leaves surface ships vulnerable to attack from hostile air and naval forces. The PLA Navy Air Force and PLA Air Force currently lack the operational range to support PLA Navy operations. In recent years, however, the PLA Navy's South Sea Fleet, which has operational responsibility over the South China Sea, has been assigned more capable surface combatants and submarines, including two destroyers (one LUDA IV class and one LUHAI class) that provide it with its first short-range area air-defense capability, the HHQ-7C surface-to-air missile systems.[78]

Joint Operations

Regarding joint operations, DOD states:

> Since 2004, the PLA has conducted a number of exercises designed to develop the PLA's joint operational concepts and demonstrate new capabilities, command automation systems, and weapons. The PLA hopes eventually to fuse service-level capabilities with an integrated network for command, control, communications, computers, intelligence, surveillance, and reconnaissance (C4ISR), a new command structure, and a joint logistics system. However, it continues to face deficiencies in inter-service cooperation and actual experience in joint operations.[79]

Another observer states:

> There is no question that China has achieved a remarkable leap in modernization of the forces needed for these missions and that it is urgently continuing on that path. There *is* question about how China is now proceeding to exercise these new assets so as to make them truly operational in a combat environment. There is *considerable question* about China's capability to coordinate all these forces in two major simultaneous operations: (1) to bring Taiwan to its knees and (2) cause the U.S. to be tardy, indecisive, or ineffective in responding.[80]

Anti-Air Warfare (AAW)

Regarding AAW, one observer states that China's decision to "shed its strictly coastal defense force structure in favor of acquiring larger and more modern fighting vessels capable of blue-water operations" has

> exposed a significant vulnerability — the PLAN's inability to provide a sophisticated, layered air defense for these new forces. Fleet air defense is the Achilles' heel of the 21st-century Chinese Navy....
>
> As the PLAN's ships increased in size, capability and endurance, and with operational deployments taking them well beyond the navy's traditional mainland-based air defenses, a challenge not faced previously became apparent: having to defend these units from air attack in the event of hostilities. Response to this concern has been slow and inadequate at best, and serious consideration to providing the surface navy with the kind of air defense systems one normally associates with modern naval fleets has only begun. Not until the late 1990s was an effort made to outfit PLAN destroyers and frigates with an antiair "point defense" system, giving them some measure of self-defense.... The PLAN surface fleet, however, still lacks "modern air surveillance systems and data links required for area air defense missions. The combination of short-range weapons and lack of modern surveillance systems limits the PLAN to self-defense and point-defense [AAW] only. As a result, except in unusual circumstances, no PLAN ship is capable of conducting air defense of another ship."[81]
>
> In a similar vein, today's PLAN naval aviation forces alone cannot provide fighter coverage for the entire Chinese coast or the fleet, so interceptor duties have ben distributed by region between naval aviation units and the PLA Air Force. This increases the number of assets available for the task, but questions remain about joint patrolling, separate chains of command, and air force over-water proficiency. When faced with training scenarios that incorporated factors likely found in a modern air combat environment, such as electronic countermeasures or even inclement weather, neither service was up to the task. In

light of these facts, the potential effectiveness of the cooperation between the two services is doubtful.

Significant gaps exist in the present PLAN fleet air defense posture. Given the forces available today, China cannot adequately defend its fleet from air attack in the modern air threat environment.[82]

Antisubmarine Warfare (ASW)

Regarding ASW, one observer states:

> The most serious deficiency of the PLAN is certainly in the area of Anti-Submarine Warfare. Good submarines, like the "Kilo" class and (possibly) the forthcoming Type-093, will play an important ASW role, but the lack of maritime patrol aircraft and of surface ships equipped with advanced acoustic sensors make the Chinese vessels vulnerable for [sic] any of the foreign high-capability submarines operating in the area.[83]

Mine Countermeasures (MCM)

Regarding MCM, one observer writes that for the PLA Navy a

> serious operational deficiency involves the mine countermeasures vessels (MCMV). Though China has an intense shipping [sic] along its coasts, the PLAN has virtually no mine-sweeping or mine-hunting capabilities. This was due, perhaps, to the consideration that the U.S. Navy is usually more concerned to keep the sea lanes open, instead of laying mines, but nevertheless the lack of MCM is simply stunning. Any hostile organisation (including, but not limited to, state-sponsored terrorists and insurgents) could play havoc with the Chinese shipping simply by laying a few mines here and there.[84]

Logistics

Regarding logistics, DOD stated in 2005:

> Since 2000, China has improved the structure, material coordination, and efficiency of its joint logistics system. However, the command system is still not compatible with the support system, and organization and planning is incompatible with supply management. The first experimental joint logistics unit was created only in July 2004.[85]

Regarding logistic support of China's new destroyers, one observer states:

The ships' new sensors, missiles and combat systems are mainly of Russian and Western origin. However, China now is faced with the challenge of operating and maintaining these advanced systems to create a credible threat to foreign navies in Far Eastern waters....

Every piece of equipment [on China's Sovremenny-class destroyers] from hull, mechanical and electrical (HM and E) technologies to guns, sonar, communications, electronic countermeasures (ECM) and missiles are totally new to the PLAN.... [For these ships,] China is dependent on Russian advisers for training, operations and maintenance. These ships largely remain in the Russian support cocoon in Dinghai rather than at a fleet base....

Isolation from other ships and crews hurts fleet integration and coordinated operations.... It is no coincidence that the Sovremnyi and Kilo submarine home bases are in an enclave of Russian support in an isolated area near the Eastern Fleet headquarters at Ningbo.

It is unlikely that Russian advisers would be onboard during actual combat operations against Taiwan and U.S. Navy air, surface and subsurface threats. PLAN officers and crew are not expected to be able to handle operations when under fire, sustaining hits and suffering system degradation or loss. This could include problems in night or rough weather environment as well. Because all of the combat systems, except for three noted, are modern Russian equipments, China has minimal capability even to repair peacetime losses in port....

A comparison [of the AAW system on the Luyang II class destroyers] to [the] U.S. Navy Aegis [combat system] is inevitable, but Aegis was on [the U.S. Navy test ship] Norton Sound for nine years of development testing prior to the first installation on the USS Ticonderoga (CG-47) 20 years ago. Developing the software for signal processing and tracking a hundred air, surface and submarine targets will take even longer for China. Integration to various indigenous ship guns and missiles and other sensors, as well as other ships' data management and weapons, will take longer. These Chinese "Aegis" ships may be limited to 1940s era radar tasks of detecting and tracking air and surface targets for their own ship weapons. Further in the future will be an 8,000-ton DDG that is predicted to be a true area-control warship with additional Aegis capabilities. It is now in early construction stages in the new Dalian shipyard.

What kind of record is provided by prior Chinese built warships with imported Russian and Western technology? These include sensors, fire control, weapons and communications as well as HM and E. The Chinese new-construction DDGs are a mix of local designed and manufactured systems, foreign imports with production rights, illegally copied import equipment and illegal examples with no local production capability at all. The latter two represent serious training and maintenance problems. Unfortunately for the PLAN, some of them are in the highest mission-critical areas. For example, the DDGs being built have a rapid-fire Gatling gun close-in weapon system that looks like the Dutch Goalkeeper system. Signaal and the Dutch government deny exporting the equipment or production rights to China. This key weapon responsible for downing incoming cruise missiles is probably lacking documentation and training because it must be illegally obtained.[86]

Goals or Significance of China's Naval Modernization

PLA Navy as a Modernization Priority

The PLA Navy is one of three stated priorities within China's overall military modernization effort. China's 2004 defense white paper says three times that the effort will emphasize the navy, air force, and the ballistic missile force.[87] China's 2006 defense white paper states: "Through restructuring, the proportion of the Navy, Air Force and Second Artillery Force in the PLA has been raised by 3.8 percent while that of the Army has been lowered by 1.5 percent."[88] The 2006 white paper further states:

> The Navy aims at gradual extension of the strategic depth for offshore defensive operations and enhancing its capabilities in integrated maritime operations and nuclear counterattacks....
>
> The Navy and Air Force have cut some ship groups and aviation divisions, regiments and stations, and set up some high-tech surface ship, aviation and ground-to-air missile units....
>
> The Navy is working to build itself into a modern maritime force of operation consisting of combined arms with both nuclear and conventional means of operations. Taking informationization as the goal and strategic focus in its modernization drive, the Navy gives high priority to the development of maritime information systems, and new-generation weaponry and equipment. Efforts are being made to improve maritime battlefield capabilities, with emphasis on the construction of relevant facilities for new equipment and the development of combat support capabilities. The Navy is endeavoring to build mobile maritime troops capable of conducting operations under conditions of informationization, and strengthen its overall capabilities of operations in coastal waters, joint operations and integrated maritime support. Efforts are being made to improve and reform training programs and methods to intensify training in joint integrated maritime operations. The Navy is enhancing research into the theory of naval operations and exploring the strategy and tactics of maritime people's war under modern conditions.[89]

The heads of the PLA Navy, Air Force, and missile force were added to the Central Military Commission in September 2004, and Navy and Air Force officers were appointed Deputy Chiefs of the General Staff.[90] Regarding this development, a 2007 report from the Office of Naval Intelligence states:

> In September 2004, the commander of the PLAN, Admiral Zhang Dingfa, became the first PLAN commander ever to serve concurrently as a member of the CCP Central Committee's Military Commission (CMC). His promotion in grade and appointment to the CMC provided a unique challenge for the PLAN within the PLA hierarchy.
>
> [A]ll organizations within the PLA are assigned one of 15 grades. In addition, the commander and political officer are assigned the same grade. However, when Zhang Dingfa was promoted one grade as a CMC member, neither the grade for the PLAN as an organization nor the grade of the PLAN political commissar was raised to the same level. Therefore, although Zhang and his successors will hold the same grade as the Chief of the General Staff and the directors of the General Political Department (GPD), General Logistics Department (GLD), and General Equipment Department (GED), the PLAN as an organization is not equal to the four General Departments and is still at the same grade as the seven Military Regions.[91]

Near-Term Focus: Taiwan Situation

DOD and other observers believe that the near-term focus of China's military modernization is to develop military options for addressing the situation with Taiwan. DOD lists China's potential military options regarding Taiwan as follows:

- limited force options that "could include computer network attacks against Taiwan's political, military, and economic infrastructure to undermine the Taiwan population's confidence in its leadership. PLA special operations forces infiltrated into Taiwan could conduct acts of economic, political, and military sabotage. Beijing might also employ SRBM, special operations forces, and air strikes against air fields, radars, and communications facilities on Taiwan....";
- an air and missile campaign, in which "Surprise SRBM attacks and precision air strikes against Taiwan's air defense system, including air bases, radar sites, missiles, space assets, and communications facilities could support a campaign to degrade Taiwan defenses neutralize its military and political leadership, and rapidly break its

will to fight while attempting to preclude an effective international response;"
- a blockade, in which "Beijing could threaten or deploy a naval blockade as a "non-war" pressure tactic in the pre-hostility phase or as a transition to active conflict. Beijing could declare that ships en route to Taiwan ports must stop in mainland ports for inspections prior to transiting on to Taiwan. It could also attempt the equivalent of a blockade by declaring exercise or missile closure areas in approaches and roadsteads to ports to divert merchant traffic, as occurred during the 1995-96 missile firings and live-fire exercises. Chinese doctrine also includes activities such as air blockades, missile attacks, and mining or otherwise obstructing harbors and approaches. More traditional blockades would have greater impact on Taiwan, but tax PLA Navy capabilities. Any attempt to limit maritime traffic to and from Taiwan would likely trigger countervailing international pressure, and risk military escalation. Such restrictions would have immediate economic effects, but would take time to realize decisive political results, diminishing the ultimate effectiveness and inviting international reaction;"[92] and
- an amphibious invasion, about which DOD states that "Publicly available Chinese writings offer different strategies... the most prominent being the Joint Island Landing Campaign. The Joint Island Landing Campaign envisions a complex operation relying on supporting sub-campaigns for logistics, electronic warfare, and air and naval support, to break through or circumvent shore defenses, establish and build a beachhead, and then launch an attack to split, seize, and occupy the entire island or key targets.[93]

Anti-Access Force for Short-Duration Conflict

More specifically, observers believe that China's military modernization is aimed at fielding a force that can succeed in a short-duration conflict with Taiwan that finishes before the United States is able to intervene, so that China can present the United States and the rest of the world with a *fait accompli*.[94]

Consistent with the goal of a short-duration conflict and a *fait accompli*, observers believe, China wants its modernized military to be capable of acting as a so-called anti-access force — a force that can deter U.S. intervention, or failing that, delay the arrival or reduce the effectiveness of U.S. intervention forces, particularly

U.S. Navy forces. DOD states that "If a quick resolution [to a situation involving Taiwan] is not possible, Beijing would seek to deter U.S. intervention or, failing that, delay such intervention, defeat it in an asymmetric, limited, quick war; or, fight it to a standstill and pursue a protracted conflict."[95] DOD also states that:

> In the near term, China is prioritizing measures to deter or counter third-party intervention in any future cross-Strait crises. China's approach to dealing with this challenge centers on what DoD's 2006 Quadrennial Defense Review report refers to as disruptive capabilities: forces and operational concepts aimed at preventing an adversary from deploying military forces to forward operating locations, and/or rapidly destabilizing critical military balances. In this context, the PLA appears engaged in a sustained effort to develop the capability to interdict, at long ranges, aircraft carrier and expeditionary strike groups that might deploy to the western Pacific. Increasingly, China's area denial/anti-access forces overlap, providing multiple layers of offensive systems, utilizing the sea, air, and space....
>
> The PLA envisions precision strike capabilities sufficient to hold at risk western Pacific airbases, ports, surface combatants, land and space-based C4ISR, air defense systems, and command facilities.
>
> To prevent deployment of naval forces into western Pacific waters, PLA planners are focused on targeting surface ships at long ranges. Analyses of current and projected force structure improvements suggest that in the near term, China is seeking the capacity to hold surface ships at risk through a layered defense that reaches out to the "second island chain" (i.e., the islands extending south and east from Japan, to and beyond Guam in the western Pacific Ocean). One area of apparent investment emphasis involves a combination of medium-range ballistic missiles, C4ISR for geo-location of targets, and onboard guidance systems for terminal homing to strike surface ships on the high seas or their onshore support infrastructure. This capability would have particular significance, owing to the preemptive and coercive options it would provide China in a regional crisis.
>
> Chinese military analysts have also concluded that logistics and mobilization are potential vulnerabilities in modern warfare, given the heavy requirements for precisely coordinated transportation, communications, and logistics networks. To threaten in-theater bases and logistics points, China could employ its theater ballistic missiles, land-attack cruise missiles, special operations forces, and computer network attacks. Strike aircraft, enabled by aerial refueling, could engage distant targets using air-launched cruise missiles equipped with a variety of terminal-homing warheads.

Advanced mines, submarines, maritime strike aircraft, and modern surface combatants equipped with advanced ASCMs would provide a supporting layer of defense for its long-range anti-access systems. Acquisition of the KILO, SONG, SHANG, and YUAN-class submarines illustrates the importance the PLA places on undersea warfare. The purchase of SOVREMENNYY II-class DDGs and indigenous production of the LUYANG I/LUYANG II DDGs equipped with long-range ASCM and SAM systems demonstrate a continuing emphasis on improving anti-surface warfare, combined with mobile, wide-area air control.[96]

Regarding the potential time line for a short-duration conflict with Taiwan, one observer states:

> The U.S. (particularly the U.S. Pacific Command/PACOM) seems to want Taiwan to focus on [acquiring] systems and defensive operational capabilities that would lengthen the amount of time Taiwan could deny the PRC from gaining air superiority, sea control, and physical occupation of Taiwan's leadership core (namely Taipei). The idea is to permit sufficient time to bring U.S. forces to bear. The amount of time needed is understood to be at least 5 days, presumably after credible warning that hostilities either are imminent or are already underway.[97]

China's emerging maritime anti-access force can be viewed as broadly analogous to the sea-denial force that the Soviet Union developed during the Cold War to deny U.S. use of the sea or counter U.S. forces participating in a NATO-Warsaw Pact conflict. One potential difference between the Soviet sea-denial force and China's emerging maritime anti-access force is that China's force could include MaRV-equipped TBMs capable of hitting moving ships at sea.

Some analysts speculate that China may attain (or believe that is has attained) a capable maritime anti-access capability, or important elements of it, by about 2010.[98] Other observers believe China will attain (or believe that it has attained) such a capability some time after 2010. DOD states that "The Intelligence Community estimates China will take until the end of this decade or later to produce a modern force capable of defeating a moderate-size adversary."[99] The term "moderate-size adversary" would appear to apply to a country other than the United States. The issue of when China might attain (or believe that it has attained) a capable anti-access capability is significant because it can influence the kinds of options that are available to U.S. policymakers for addressing the situation.

Broader or Longer-Term Regional Goals

In addition to the near-term focus on developing military options for addressing the situation with Taiwan, DOD and some other observers believe that broader or longer-term goals of China's military modernization, including naval modernization, include one or more of the following:

- asserting China's regional military leadership, displacing U.S. regional military influence, prevailing in regional rivalries, and encouraging eventual U.S. military withdrawal form the region;
- defending China's claims in maritime territorial disputes, some of which have implications for oil, gas, or mineral exploration rights;[100] and
- protecting China's sea lines of communication, which China relies upon increasingly for oil and other imports.[101]

DOD states that:

> China's near-term focus on preparing for military contingencies in the Taiwan Strait, including the possibility of U.S. intervention, appears to be an important driver of its modernization plans. However, analysis of China's military acquisitions and strategic thinking suggests Beijing is also generating capabilities for other regional contingencies, such as conflict over resources or territory.[102]

Similarly, DOD states that:

> For the moment, China's military is focused on assuring the capability to prevent Taiwan independence and, if Beijing were to decide to adopt such an approach, to compel the island to negotiate a settlement on Beijing's terms. At the same time, China is laying the foundation for a force able to accomplish broader regional and global objectives.[103]

DOD also states that:

> As China's economy grows, dependence on secure access to markets and natural resources, particularly metals and fossil fuels, is becoming a more urgent influence on China's strategic behavior. At present, China can neither protect its foreign energy supplies nor the routes on which they travel, including the Straits of Malacca through which some 80 percent of China's cruse oil imports transit

— a vulnerability [Chinese] President Hu refers to as the "Malacca Dilemma."...

China's reliance on foreign energy imports has affected its strategy and policy in significant ways. It has pursued long-term energy supply agreements in [various countries]...

In the past few years, China has also offered economic assistance and military cooperation with countries located astride key maritime transit routes. Concern over these routes has also prompted China to pursue maritime capabilities that would help it ensure the safe passage of resources through international waterways.[104]

DOD further states that:

The principal focus of, and driver for, China's military modernization in the near term appears to remain preparing for potential conflict in the Taiwan Strait. However, official documents and the writings of Chinese military strategists suggest Beijing is increasingly surveying the strategic landscape beyond Taiwan. Some Chinese analysts have explored the geopolitical value of Taiwan in extending China's maritime "defensive" perimeter and improving its ability to influence regional sea lines of communication....

China's 2006 Defense White Paper similarly raises concerns about resources and transportation links when it states that "security issues related to energy, resources, finance, information, and international shipping routes are mounting."... Disagreements that remain with Japan over maritime claims and with several Southeast Asian claimants to all or parts of the Spratly Islands in the South China Sea could lead to renewed tensions in these areas....

Analysis of China's weapons acquisitions also suggests China is looking beyond Taiwan as it builds its force. For example, new missile units outfitted with conventional theater-range missiles at various locations in China could be used in a variety of non-Taiwan contingencies. Airborne early warning and control and aerial-refueling programs will permit extended air operations into the South China Sea. Advanced destroyers and submarines reflect Beijing's desire to protect and advance its maritime interests. Expeditionary forces (three airborne divisions, two amphibious infantry divisions, two marine brigades, about seven special operations groups, and one regimental-size reconnaissance element in the Second Artillery) are improving with the introduction of new equipment, better unit-level tactics, and greater coordination of joint operations. Over the long term, improvements in China's C4ISR, including space-based and over-the-horizon sensors, could enable Beijing to identify, track and target military activities deep into the western Pacific Ocean.

Finally, analysis of PLA training activities provides an additional indication that the PLA is exploring contingencies other than Taiwan.[105]

In January 2007, the Director of National Intelligence stated:

> Beijing continues its rapid rate of military modernization, initiated in 1999. We assess that China's aspirations for great power status, threat perceptions, and security strategy would drive this modernization effort even if the Taiwan problem were resolved.[106]

A 2007 report by a task force sponsored by the Council on Foreign Relations stated:

> China's military modernization has two main drivers, one with a clear operational objective (Taiwan) and the other with a clear strategic objective (to build a modern military because China will be a modern power).[107]

Another observer states:

> While committed to deterring or defeating Taiwan and thwarting U.S. intervention, the PLAN's focus increasingly represents a more general — and ambitious — goal of attaining the means of projecting power across the sea lines of communication (SLOC) and protecting the ocean commerce on which China's economy relies. Such an objective explains certain aspects of its modernization, such as the aggressive construction of a new class of nuclear attack submarines (SSNs). The successful development of the SSNs would allow the PLAN to deter would-be disrupters of Chinese energy supplies, the majority of which are transported by sea. Moreover, sea-lane security presents a rationale for the development of an aircraft carrier, a type of ship that would serve only as an easy target in a Taiwan scenario — where China's land-based airfields are more than sufficient — but would allow for the Chinese military to project its power across maritime regions far beyond the range of land-based aircraft.
>
> Indeed, these developments indicate that China's senior leaders and strategists are increasingly concerned with traditional and non-traditional threats (e.g. piracy, smuggling, terrorism and other disruptions by non-state actors) to [108] ocean commerce.

Some PLA Navy units have recently been deployed outside China's home waters. In November 2004, for example, a Han-class SSN was detected in Japanese territorial waters near Okinawa.[109] DIA states that, as part of the same deployment, this submarine traveled "far into the western Pacific Ocean...."[110] Press reports state that the submarine operated in the vicinity of Guam before moving toward Okinawa.[111]

As another example, on September 9, 2005,

China deployed a fleet of five warships... near a gas field in the East China Sea, a potentially resource-rich area that is disputed by China and Japan. The ships, including a guided-missile destroyer, were spotted by a Japanese military patrol plane near the Chunxiao gas field, according to the [Japan] Maritime Self-Defense Forces.[112]

As a third example,

China said on Sept. 29 [of 2005 that] it has sent warships to the disputed East China Sea, a day ahead of talks with Japan over competing territorial claims in the gas-rich waters.
"I can now confirm that in the East China Sea, a Chinese reserve vessel squadron has been established," foreign ministry spokesman Qin Gang told a regular briefing....
No details were given on the size of the squadron or the area it will patrol. The establishment of the squadron follows China's creation of two naval groups in the Bohai Sea and Yellow Sea off the northern China coast, the agency said.[113]

On October 26, 2006, a Song-class SS reportedly surfaced five miles away from the Japan-homeported U.S. Navy aircraft carrier Kitty Hawk (CV-63), which reportedly was operating at the time with its strike group in international waters in the East China Sea, near Okinawa. According to press reports, the carrier strike group at the time was not actively searching for submarines, and the Song-class boat remained undetected by the strike group until it surfaced and was observed by one of the strike group's aircraft.[114] The Chinese government denied that the submarine was following the strike group.[115]

A distance of five miles would be well within the typical defensive perimeter for a carrier strike group. (Such a perimeter might extend tens of miles, or more than 100 miles, from a strike group's ships.) It would also be within the reported firing range of certain modern submarine-launched torpedoes, and well within the firing range of submarine-launched ASCMs.

The surfacing of an undetected submarine well within the defensive perimeter of another country's surface naval formation can sometimes be intended as a deterrent action — a warning from the submarine-operating country that submarines like the one in question can penetrate the ASW systems of the other country's surface naval forces. Whether that was the intent behind the Song-class boat's decision to surface is not clear; the boat may have surfaced for other reasons. Since the Kitty Hawk strike group was not actively searching for submarines at the time, the implications of the incident for assessing U.S. ASW capabilities against Song-class submarines are also not clear. U.S. officials reportedly will review their ASW defenses in light of the incident.[116]

Regarding base access and support facilities to support more distant PLA Navy operations, one press report states:

> China is building up military forces and setting up bases along sea lanes from the Middle East to project its power overseas and protect its oil shipments, according to a previously undisclosed internal report prepared for Defense Secretary Donald H. Rumsfeld.
>
> "China is building strategic relationships along the sea lanes from the Middle East to the South China Sea in ways that suggest defensive and offensive positioning to protect China's energy interests, but also to serve broad security objectives," said the report sponsored by the director, Net Assessment, who heads Mr. Rumsfeld's office on future-oriented strategies.
>
> The Washington Times obtained a copy of the report, titled "Energy Futures in Asia," which was produced by defense contractor Booz Allen Hamilton.
>
> The internal report stated that China is adopting a "string of pearls" strategy of bases and diplomatic ties stretching from the Middle East to southern China....[117]

POTENTIAL IMPLICATIONS FOR REQUIRED U.S. NAVY CAPABILITIES

Potential implications of China's naval modernization for required U.S. Navy capabilities can be organized into three groups:

- capabilities for a crisis or conflict in the Taiwan Strait area;
- capabilities for maintaining U.S. Navy presence and military influence in the Western Pacific; and
- operating an eavesdropping post and building a naval base at Gwadar, Pakistan, near the Persian Gulf;
- building a container port facility at Chittagong, Bangladesh, and seeking "much more extensive naval and commercial access" in Bangladesh;
- building naval bases in Burma, which is near the Strait of Malacca;
- operating electronic intelligence-gathering facilities on islands in the Bay of Bengal and near the Strait of Malacca;
- building a railway line from China through Cambodia to the sea;

- improving its ability to project air and sea power into the South China Sea from mainland China and Hainan Island;
- considering funding a $20-billion canal that would cross the Kra Isthmus of Thailand, which would allow ships to bypass the Strait of Malacca and permit China to establish port facilities there.
- capabilities for detecting, tracking, and if necessary countering PLA Navy SSBNs equipped with long-range SLBMs.

Each of these is discussed below.

Capabilities for Taiwan Strait Crisis or Conflict

U.S. military operations in a potential crisis or conflict in the Taiwan Strait area would likely feature a strong reliance on U.S. Navy forces and land-based U.S. Air Force aircraft.[118] If air bases in Japan and South Korea are, for political reasons, not available to the United States for use in the operation, or if air bases in Japan, South Korea, or Guam are rendered less useful by PLA attacks using TBMs, LACMs, or special operations forces, then the reliance on U.S. Navy forces could become greater.

For the U.S. Navy, a crisis or conflict in the Taiwan Strait could place a premium on the following:

- on-station or early-arriving forces;
- forces with a capability to defeat PLA anti-access weapons and platforms;
- forces with an ability to operate in an environment that could be characterized by IW/IO and possibly EMP or the use of nuclear weapons directly against Navy ships; and
- forces that can be ready to conduct operations by about 2010, or by some later date.

On-Station and Early-Arriving Forces

In the scenario of a short-duration conflict, on-station and early-arriving U.S. Navy forces could be of particular value, while later-arriving U.S. Navy forces might be of less value, at least in preventing initial success by PLA forces.

On-Station Forces

Given the difficulty of knowing with certainty when a Taiwan Strait crisis or conflict might occur, having forces on-station at the start of the crisis or conflict is a goal that would most reliably be met by maintaining a standing forward deployment of U.S. Navy forces in the area. Maintaining a standing forward deployment of U.S. Navy forces in the area while also maintaining U.S. Navy forward deployments in other regions, such as the Persian Gulf/Indian Ocean region and the Mediterranean Sea, would require a Navy with a certain minimum number of ships.

Although it is sometimes said that it takes three U.S. Navy ships to keep one ship forward deployed in an overseas location, the actual ratio traditionally has been higher. For example, if U.S. Navy ships are operated in the traditional manner — with a single crew for each ship and deployments lasting six months — then maintaining one U.S. Navy cruiser or destroyer continuously forward-deployed to the Western Pacific might require a total of about five San Diego-based cruisers or destroyers.[119]

Stationkeeping multipliers like these can be reduced by homeporting U.S. Navy ships at locations closer to Taiwan (such as Japan, Guam, Hawaii, or perhaps Singapore) or by deploying ships for longer periods of time and operating them with multiple crews that are rotated out to each ship. The Navy has an aircraft carrier strike group and other ships[120] homeported in Japan, and three attack submarines homeported in Guam.[121] The Navy has also experimented with the concept of deploying certain Navy ships (particularly surface combatants) for 12, 18, or 24 months and rotating multiple crews out to each ship.[122]

Early-Arriving Forces

Having early-arriving U.S. Navy forces could mean having forces based in locations Western Pacific locations such as Japan, Guam, Singapore, or perhaps Hawaii, rather than on the U.S. West Coast.[123] Table 5 shows potential ship travel times to the Taiwan Strait area from various ports in the Pacific, based on average ship travel speeds. All the ports shown in the table except Singapore are current U.S. Navy home ports.[124] U.S. Navy submarines, aircraft carriers, cruisers, and destroyers have maximum sustained speeds of more than 30 knots, but their average speeds over longer transits in some cases might be closer to 25 knots or less due rough sea conditions or, in the case of the cruisers or destroyers, which are conventionally powered, the need slow down for at-sea refueling.

The Navy's Littoral Combat Ship (LCS) is to have a maximum sustained speed of about 45 knots, but its average speed over long transits would likely be less than that.

As can be seen in the table, Yokosuka, Guam, and Singapore are less than half as far from the Taiwan Strait area as are Pearl Harbor, Everett, WA,[125] and San Diego. Depending on their average travel speeds, ships homeported in Yokosuka, Guam, and Singapore could arrive in the Taiwan Strait area roughly two to four days after leaving port, ships homeported in Pearl Harbor might arrive about six to nine days after leaving port, and ships homeported on the U.S. West Coast might arrive about 7 to 12 days after leaving port. The time needed to get a ship and its crew ready to leave port would add to their total response times. Depending on a ship's status at the moment it was ordered to the Taiwan Strait area, preparing it for rapid departure might require anywhere from less than one day to a few days.

Table 5. Potential Ship Travel Times to Taiwan Strait Area

Port	Straight-line distance to Taiwan Strait area[a] (nautical miles)	Minimum travel time in days, based on average speeds below[b] 20 knots	25 knots	30 knots
Yokosuka, Japan[c]	1,076	2.2	1.8	1.5
Guam	1,336	2.8	2.2	1.9
Singapore[d]	1,794	3.7	3.0	2.5
Pearl Harbor[e]	4,283	8.9	7.1	5.9
Everett, WA	5,223	10.9	8.7	7.3
San Diego	5,933	12.3	9.9	8.2

Source: Table prepared by CRS using straight-line distances calculated by the "how far is it" calculator, available at [http://www.indo.com/distance/].

a. Defined as a position in the sea at $24°N$, $124°E$, which is roughly 130 nautical miles *east* of Taiwan, i.e., on the other side of Taiwan from the Taiwan Strait.
b. Actual travel times may be greater due to the possible need for ships to depart from a straight-line course so as to avoid land barriers, remain within port-area shipping channels, etc.
c. Distance calculated from Tokyo, which is about 25 nautical miles north of Yokosuka.
d. No U.S. Navy ships are currently homeported at Singapore.
e. Distance calculated from Honolulu, which is about 6 nautical miles southeast of Pearl Harbor.

Regarding the possibility of transferring of a carrier from the continental United States to Hawaii or Guam — an option that DOD considered in 2005-2006 but decided against in 2007[126] — one observer states:

Currently the United States maintains one aircraft carrier full-time in the Western Pacific. In the event of a conflict with China over Taiwan, however, particularly given the various [PLA] threats to land-based air outlined above, having more aircraft carriers on the scene will be extremely valuable. Other than any carriers that might be transiting through the region, however, currently the closest additional carriers would be those based on the west coast of the United States. Given that a conflict with China could begin with little warning, this means that as much as two weeks could elapse before additional aircraft carriers reached the area of combat operations. The Department of Defense has already recommended forward-deploying an additional aircraft carrier in the Pacific, but it is important to note that precisely where this carrier is forward-deployed is significant. In particular, an aircraft carrier based in Hawaii would still take at least a week to reach waters near Taiwan. An aircraft carrier based in Guam, Singapore, or elsewhere in the Western Pacific, by contrast, could arrive on the scene in about three days.[127]

Basing additional forces in Japan, Guam, Singapore, or Hawaii could increase the importance of taking actions to defend these locations against potential attack by TBMs, LACMs, or special operations forces.[128]

Defeating PLA Anti-Access Forces

Defeating PLA maritime anti-access forces would require capabilities for countering:

- large numbers of TBMs, including some possibly equipped with MaRVs;
- large numbers of LACMs and ASCMs, including some advanced ASCMs such as the SS-N-27 and SS-N-22;
- substantial numbers of land-based fighters, strike fighters, maritime bombers, and SAMs, including some built to modern designs;
- a substantial number of submarines, including a few that are nuclear-powered and a significant portion that are built to modern designs;
- a substantial number of destroyers, frigates, and fast attack craft, including some built to modern designs; and
- potentially large numbers of mines of different types, including some advanced models.

Countering TBMs

Countering large numbers of TBMs, including some possibly equipped with MaRVs, could entail some or all of the following:

- operating, if possible, in a way that reduces the likelihood of being detected and tracked by PLA maritime surveillance systems;
- attacking the surveillance systems that detect and track U.S. Navy ships operating at sea, and the network that transmits this targeting data to the TBMs;
- attacking TBMs at their launch sites;
- intercepting TBMs in flight, which in some cases could require firing two or perhaps even three interceptor missiles at individual TBMs to ensure their destruction;
- decoying MaRVs away from U.S. Navy ships.

Potential implications of the above points for Navy missile-defense programs are discussed in this next section of this report.

Countering Submarines

Countering a substantial number of submarines would likely require a coordinated effort by an ASW network consisting of some or all of the following: distributed sensors, unmanned vehicles, submarines, surface ships, helicopters, and maritime patrol aircraft. Defeating torpedoes fired by PLA submarines would require U.S. submarines and surface ships to have systems for detecting, decoying, and perhaps destroying those torpedoes.

ASW operations against well-maintained and well-operated submarines traditionally have often been time-consuming. Acoustic conditions in at least some of the waters around Taiwan are reportedly poor for ASW, which could make the task of countering PLA submarines in these areas more difficult.[129] Success in an ASW operation is highly dependent on the proficiency of the people operating the ASW equipment. ASW operational proficiency can take time to develop and can atrophy significantly if not regularly exercised.

In December 2004, the Navy approved a new concept of operations (CONOPS) a new general approach — to ASW. As described in one article,

> The Navy's new concept of operations for anti-submarine warfare calls for the use of standoff weapons, networked sensor fields and unmanned vehicles to detect and attack diesel submarines in littoral waters, rather than a reliance on "force on force" engagements.
>
> Chief of Naval Operations Adm. Vern Clark approved the CONOPS Dec. 20, according to a Navy spokesman. The five-page document will guide the development of a comprehensive ASW master plan that is expected to be classified, though it might have an unclassified version.

The CONOPS envisions hundreds or thousands of small sensors that would "permeate the operating environment, yielding unprecedented situational awareness and highly detailed pictures of the battlespace." Attack submarines that today carry sensors and weapons could in the future provide logistical support to and serve as command and control bases for off-board sensors and "kill vehicles," the CONOPS states. The networking of autonomous sensor fields with manned and unmanned vehicles will change ASW from a "platform-intensive" to a "sensor-rich" operation, it adds.[130]

At a June 20, 2005, conference on the future of the Navy organized by the American Enterprise Institute (AEI), Admiral Vernon Clark, who was the Chief of Naval Operations until July 22, 2005, stated:

[The Chinese are] building submarines at a rapid rate. They're buying them from other countries. They're building their own capabilities. And let me just to make a long story short, I published a new ASW concept [of operations] a couple of months ago. I fundamentally don't believe that the old attrition warfare[,] force on force anti-submarine warfare[,] construct is the right way to go in the 21st century. [The questioner] mentioned that I had spent part of my past life in the submarine warfare business. I have. I trailed the Soviets around. I know what that's about. And what I really believe is going to happen in the future is that when we apply the netted force construct in anti-submarine warfare, it will change the calculus in that area of warfighting forever. And it will be a courageous commander who decides that he's going to come waltzing into our network.[131]

Implementing this new ASW concept of operations reportedly will require overcoming some technical challenges, particularly with regard to linking together large numbers of distributed sensors, some of which might be sonobuoys as small as soda cans.[132]

Countering Mines

Countering naval mines is a notoriously time-consuming task that can require meticulous operations by participating surface ships, submarines, and helicopters. The Navy's mine countermeasures (MCM) capabilities have been an area of concern in Congress and elsewhere for a number of years.[133] The Navy for the last several years has been developing several new MCM systems that are scheduled to enter service over the next few years.[134] Unmanned surface vehicles (USVs) and unmanned underwater vehicles (UUVs) are playing an increasing role in MCM operations.

Operating Amidst IW/IO, EMP, and Nuclear Weapons

Operating effectively in an environment that could be characterized by IW/IO and possibly EMP or the use of nuclear weapons directly against Navy ships could require, among other things:

- measures to achieve and maintain strong computer network security;
- hardening of ships, aircraft, and their various systems against EMP; and
- hardening of ships against the overpressure, thermal, and radiation effects of a nuclear weapon that is detonated somewhat close to the ship, but not close enough to destroy the ship outright.

Forces Ready by about 2010, or by a Later Date

As mentioned earlier, some analysts speculate that China may attain (or believe that is has attained) a capable maritime anti-access capability, or important elements of it, by about 2010, while other observers believe this will happen some time after 2010. The issue of whether or when China might attain such a capability can influence the kinds of options that are available to U.S. policymakers for addressing the situation.

Options for a Conflict Between Now and 2010

Options that could enhance U.S. Navy capabilities for a crisis or conflict in the Taiwan Strait area between now and 2010 include, among others, the following:

- increasing currently planned activities for physically surveying the physical environment around Taiwan, so as to more quickly update older data that might unreliable, and to fill in any gaps in understanding regarding how local atmospheric and water conditions might affect the performance of radars and sonars;
- increasing currently planned levels of monitoring and surveillance of PLA forces that are likely to participate in a crisis or conflict in the Taiwan Strait area;[135]
- increasing currently planned levels of contact between the U.S. Navy and Taiwan military forces, so as to maintain a fully up-to-date U.S. understanding of Taiwan military capabilities, plans, and doctrine (and vice versa);

- increasing currently planned military exercises that are tailored to the potential requirements of a crisis or conflict in the Taiwan Strait area;
- increasing the number of ships that are assigned to the Pacific Fleet, or the number that are forward-homeported at locations such as Japan, Guam, Hawaii, and perhaps Singapore, or the numbers of both;
- deferring current plans for retiring existing ships or aircraft before 2010, particularly ships and aircraft whose nominal service lives would otherwise extend to 2010 or beyond;
- modernizing ships and aircraft now in service;
- reactivating recently retired ships and aircraft;[136] and
- procuring new items that can be completed between now and 2010, such as weapons, aircraft, and Littoral Combat Ships (LCSs).

Options for a Conflict after 2010

Options that could enhance U.S. Navy capabilities for a crisis or conflict in the Taiwan Strait area some time after 2010 include items from the above list, plus the procurement of larger ships that take several years to build (e.g., SSNs, aircraft carriers, destroyers, and cruisers), and the development and procurement of aircraft and weapons that are not currently ready for procurement.

Capabilities for Maintaining Regional Presence and Influence

For the U.S. Navy, maintaining regional presence and military influence in the Western Pacific could place a premium on the following, among other things:

- maintaining a substantial U.S. Navy ship presence throughout the region;
- making frequent port calls in the region;
- conducting frequent exercises with other navies in the region;
- taking actions to ensure system compatibility between U.S. Navy ships and ships of allied and friendly nations in the region; and
- conducting frequent exchanges between U.S. Navy personnel and military and political leaders of other countries in the region.

Factors influencing the Navy's ability to maintain a substantial U.S. Navy ship presence throughout the region include the total number of ships in the Navy's Pacific Fleet, the number of Navy ships forward-homeported at locations such as Japan, Guam, Hawaii, and perhaps Singapore, and ship-crewing and -deployment approaches (e.g., six-month deployments and single crews vs. longer deployments with crew rotation).

Capabilities for Tracking and Countering PLA SSBNs

Detecting, tracking, and if necessary countering PLA Navy SSBNs equipped with long-range SLBMs could require some or all of the following:

- a seabed-based sensor network analogous to the Sound Surveillance System (SOSUS) that the U.S. Navy used during the Cold War to detect and track Soviet nuclear-powered submarines;
- ocean surveillance ships with additional sonars, which would be similar to the TAGOS-type ocean-surveillance ships that the Navy also used during the Cold War to help detect and track Soviet nuclear-powered submarines; and
- enough SSNs so that some can be assigned to tracking and if necessary attacking PLA SSBNs.[137]

Chapter 3

POTENTIAL OVERSIGHT ISSUES FOR CONGRESS

Potential oversight questions for Congress arising from China's military modernization and its potential implications for required U.S. Navy capabilities can be organized into three groups:

- questions relating to China's military modernization as a defense-planning priority;
- questions relating to U.S. Navy force structure and basing arrangements; and
- questions relating to Navy warfare areas and programs.

Each of these is discussed below.

CHINA AS A DEFENSE-PLANNING PRIORITY

DOD Planning

Is DOD giving adequate weight in its planning to China's military modernization as opposed to other concerns, such as current operations in Iraq and Afghanistan and the global war on terrorism (GWOT) generally? Is DOD giving adequate weight in its planning to the funding needs of the Navy as opposed to those of the other services, such as the Army?

Military operations in Iraq and Afghanistan have led to increased focus on the funding needs of the Army and Marine Corps, since these two services are heavily committed to those operations. Placing increasing emphasis on China in DOD planning, on the other hand, would likely lead to increased focus on the funding needs of the Navy and Air Force, since these two services are generally viewed as the ones most likely to be of the most importance for a crisis or conflict in the Taiwan Strait area. In a situation of finite DOD resources, striking the correct planning balance between operations in Iraq and Afghanistan and the GWOT generally, and China's military modernization is viewed by some observers as a key DOD planning challenge.

Navy Planning

Is the Navy is giving adequate weight in its planning to China's military modernization as opposed to other concerns, such as the GWOT?

Required Navy capabilities for participating in the GWOT overlap with, but are not identical to, required Navy capabilities for responding to China's naval modernization. In a situation of finite Navy resources, striking the correct balance between investments for participating in the GWOT and those for responding to China's naval modernization is viewed by some observers as a key Navy planning challenge.

The Navy since 2005 has implemented several organizational and programmatic initiatives that reflect an interest in increasing the Navy's role in the GWOT.[138] At the same time, the Navyhas occasionally affirmed the importance of China's military modernization in its budget planning. At a June 20, 2005 conference on the future of the Navy organized by the American Enterprise Institute (AEI), for example, Admiral Clark was asked to comment on China. He stated in part:

> Well, I think that, you know, we're always quick to point out that China's not our enemy, but China is building a very capable maritime capability, and so we should not be blind to that.
>
> So what does it mean? Well, here's what I believe that it means. I believe that if you study the Chinese, you see that there's been some change in their thinking over the course of the last number of years. Here's this mammoth land, continent; here's — you know, it would be easy to think about this country as being land-centric in terms of its national security focus, but what we're seeing is that that really isn't where they're putting their money. They're putting their investments in, and what it looks like, if you interpret their actions, is that their

primary concerns are in the area of aviation and maritime capability that other nations would bring to bear in their area, in their region of the world. And so they're trying to build a capability to make sure that they're not pushed into a corner in their own part of the world.

I understand that this morning there was conjecture about their ability to build missile systems that will threaten long-range land bases and moving targets in the future, like ships at sea. And I will tell you that whether they're going to do that or not, I guarantee you that I believe that it is my duty and responsibility to expect that, based on what I understand about what they're doing, to expect that they're trying to do that. And I will tell you that the budget submit that's on the Hill is providing the kind of capability to make sure that the United States Navy can fight in that theater or exist in that theater, understanding the kind of capability that they're trying to bring to bear.[139]

NAVY FORCE STRUCTURE AND BASING ARRANGEMENTS

Size of the Fleet

Is the Navy planning a fleet with enough ships to address potential challenges posed by China's naval modernization while also meeting other responsibilities?

As of May 11, 2007, the Navy included a total of 276 ships of various kinds. The Navy is proposing to maintain in coming years a fleet of 313 ships.[140] In assessing the adequacy of the 313-ship proposal, a key potential issue for Congress is whether it includes enough ships to address potential challenges posed by China's naval modernization while also meeting other responsibilities, including maintaining forward deployments of Navy ships in the Persian Gulf/Indian Ocean region and conducting less-frequent operations in other parts of the world, such as the Mediterranean Sea, the Caribbean, the waters around South America, and the waters off West Africa. If increased numbers of Navy ships are needed to address potential challenges posed by China's naval modernization, fewer ships might be available for meeting other responsibilities.

Some Members of Congress have expressed concern in recent years that the declining total number of ships in the Navy may make it difficult for the Navy to perform all if its various missions, at least not without putting undue stress on Navy personnel and equipment. Navy officials have responded that the proposed 313-ship Navy would be sufficient to perform the Navy's various peacetime and wartime missions.

Division of Fleet between Atlantic and Pacific

Should a greater percentage of the Navy be assigned to the Pacific Fleet? The division of the Navy's ships between the Atlantic and Pacific fleets is a longstanding question in U.S. Navy planning. Atlantic Fleet ships conduct operations in the North and South Atlantic, the Caribbean, and the Mediterranean Sea, while Pacific Fleet ships conduct operations in the Pacific Ocean, including the Western Pacific. Ships from both fleets are used to conduct operations in the Persian Gulf/Indian Ocean area. Atlantic Fleet ships homeported on the U.S. East Coast that use the Suez Canal have a shorter transit distance to the Persian Gulf than do Pacific Fleet ships homeported on the U.S. West Coast.

In recent years, roughly 45% to 47% of the Navy's ships had been assigned to the Pacific Fleet, including 46% to 50% of the Navy's SSNs and 45% to 48% of the Navy's cruisers, destroyers, and frigates. Increasing the share of the Navy assigned to the Pacific Fleet could, other things held equal, permit the Navy to maintain a larger number of ships forward deployed to the Western Pacific. Using the size of the Navy as of the end of FY2005 (282 ships, including 54 SSNs and 99 cruisers, destroyers, and frigates), increasing the Pacific Fleet's share by 5 or 10 percentage points would result in the Pacific fleet having an additional 14 to 28 ships, including roughly 3 to 5 SSNs and roughly 5 to 10 to cruisers, destroyers, and frigates.

The final report on the 2005 Quadrennial Defense Review (QDR) directed the Navy to "to adjust its force posture and basing to provide at least six operationally available and sustainable carriers and 60% of its submarines in the Pacific to support engagement, presence and deterrence."[141]

Supporters of shifting a greater share of the Navy to the Pacific Fleet could argue that responding to China's naval modernization requires, among other things, maintaining an increased number of ships forward deployed to the Western Pacific, and that the low likelihood of war in Europe and the ability of U.S. allies in Europe to deploy their own ships to the Mediterranean reduces the number of ships that the Navy needs to maintain there. Opponents of this option could argue that shifting Navy ships from the U.S. East Coast to the U.S. West Coast could make it harder to maintain deployments of a given number of ships to the Persian Gulf (due to the increase in transit distance to the Gulf for ships transferred from the East Coast to the West Coast) and could make it more difficult for the Navy to balance the maintenance demands of the fleet against the locations of repair and overhaul yards, many of which are located on the Atlantic and Gulf coasts.

Forward Homeporting in the Western Pacific

Is the Navy moving quickly enough to forward-homeport additional ships in the Western Pacific? Should the Navy expand the number of additional ships it is thinking of homeporting in the area?

Increasing the number of ships forward homeported in the Western Pacific can increase both the number of ships that the Navy can maintain forward-deployed to that area on a day to day basis, and the number that can arrive in the early stages of a conflict in the Western Pacific, including the Taiwan Strait area. Observers who are concerned about deterring or responding to a conflict in the Taiwan Strait area by 2010 might emphasize the importance of implementing these actions as quickly as possible. They might also argue in favor of expanding the number of ships to be transferred to Western Pacific home ports. These additional ships could include SSNs, converted Trident cruise missile submarines (SSGNs), surface combatants, and perhaps one more aircraft carrier (i.e., a carrier beyond the one that the Navy reportedly is already considering transferring to Hawaii or Guam). A 2002 Congressional Budget Office (CBO) report discussed the option of homeporting a total of up to 11 SSNs at Guam.[142] Expanding the number of ships to be homeported in the Western Pacific could require construction of additional homeporting facilities, particularly in locations such as Guam. Transferring ships from the U.S. West Coast to the Western Pacific can also have implications for crew training and ship maintenance for those ships.

Number of Aircraft Carriers

How many aircraft carriers should the Navy include? The Navy's proposal for a 313-ship fleet includes 11, and eventually 12, aircraft carriers. The issue of how many carriers the Navy should operate is discussed at some length in another CRS report.[143] Advocates of maintaining a force of at least 11 carriers could argue that, in light of China's naval modernization, including the introduction of new land-based fighters and strike fighters and the possibility that the PLA might, as part of a conflict in the Taiwan Strait area, use TBMs, LACMs, or special operations forces to attack U.S. land bases in the Western Pacific, a force of at least 11 carriers is needed to deter or prevail in such a conflict. Those supporting a reduction in the carrier force to fewer than 11 ships could argue that such a reduction is acceptable in light of the increasing capabilities of individual Navy carrier air wings, the Navy's plan to transfer an additional carrier to the Western Pacific, and options for improving the defenses of U.S. bases in the Western Pacific against attack from TBMs, LACMs, and special operations forces.

Number of Attack Submarines (SSNs)

Should the number of nuclear-powered attack submarines be 48, or some other number? The Navy at the end of FY2006 operated a total of 55 SSNs. The Navy's proposal for a 313-ship fleet includes 48 SSNs (plus four converted Trident cruise missile submarines, or SSGNs). Supporters of SSNs have argued that China's naval modernization, and in particular China's submarine modernization, is a significant reason for supporting a force of 48 or more SSNs. The issue of the SSN force-level goal is discussed at length in another CRS report.[144]

Although discussion of the proper future size of the U.S. SSN force is sometimes cast in terms of U.S. SSNs fighting PLA Navy submarines, this captures only a part of how U.S. SSNs would fit into potential U.S. Navy operations against PLA forces. On the one hand, ASW is conducted by platforms other than SSNs, and an SSN is not always the best platform for countering an enemy submarine. On the other hand, SSNs perform a number of potentially significant missions other than ASW.

Supporters of maintaining 48 or more SSNs in light of China's naval modernization could argue that, in addition to participating in operations against PLA Navy submarines, U.S. SSNs could do the following:

- Conduct pre-crisis covert intelligence, surveillance, and reconnaissance (ISR) of PLA Navy forces and bases. Such operations could improve U.S. understanding PLA capabilities and weaknesses.
- Covertly lay mines around China's naval bases. In light of the PLA Navy's limited mine countermeasures capabilities, the presence of mines around PLA Navy bases could significantly delay the deployment of PLA Navy forces at the outset of a crisis or conflict.
- Attack or threaten PLA Navy surface ships. In light of the PLA Navy's limitations in ASW, a threat from U.S. SSNs could substantially complicate PLA military planning, particularly for an intended short-duration conflict.
- Fire Tomahawk cruise missiles from unexpected locations. Tomahawks could be used to attack on PLA command and control nodes, air bases, and TBM, LACM, ASCM, and SAM launch sites.
- Covertly insert and recover special operations forces (SOF). SOF can be used to attack PLA Navy bases or other PLA coastal facilities.

Supporters of maintaining 48 or more SSNs could also argue that submerged U.S. SSNs cannot be attacked by conventionally armed TBMs and ASCMs and are less vulnerable than are U.S. Navy surface ships to EMP effects and to certain other nuclear weapon effects.

Supporters of maintaining fewer than 48 SSNs could argue that U.S. SSNs, though very capable for performing certain missions, they are less capable for performing others. U.S. SSNs, they can argue, cannot shoot down enemy missiles or aircraft, nor can they act as platforms for operating manned aircraft. U.S. cruisers and destroyers, they could argue, carry substantial numbers of Tomahawks. In light of the complementary capabilities of Navy platforms and the need for an array of U.S. Navy capabilities in operations against PLA forces, they could argue, the need for SSNs needs to be balanced against the need for aircraft carriers and surface combatants.

One set of observers states that China's new nuclear-powered submarines:

> are entering the PLA Navy (PLAN) at a time when reductions are projected to occur in the U.S. Navy submarine force; that fact was duly noted by a senior PLAN strategist recently in one of China's premier naval journals.[145]

These same observers state that:

> Chinese researchers display intimate familiarity with all U.S. Navy submarine force programs, including the most cutting-edge platforms, such as Seawolf and Virginia. Additionally, there is great interest in the ongoing transformation of some SSBNs into SSGNs. Ample focus is also devoted to the capabilities of the Los Angeles class as the backbone of the U.S. Navy submarine force. Beyond platforms and programs, there is also a keen interest in America's industrial organization for nuclear submarine production and maintenance.[146]

These observers also state that:

> Chinese analysts acknowledge that America has long been dominant in undersea warfare, especially after the Cold War. Many Westerners are therefore surprised that China would have the temerity to challenge the United States directly in this specialized domain of warfare. Yet PLAN analysts keep close tabs on U.S. Navy submarine building rates and carefully probe for potential American submarine force vulnerabilities. They have studied the 8 January 2005 accident involving [the Los Angeles-class SSN] USS San Francisco[147] with great interest. A 2006 article by a senior PLAN strategist suggests that "China already exceeds [U.S. submarine production] five times over" and that eighteen U.S. Navy submarines based in the Pacific might be at a severe disadvantage

against seventy-five or more Chinese submarines. While these assessments are ultimately attributed to an American source, the PLAN analyst makes no effort to deny or reject these assessments.[148]

ASW-Capable Ships and Aircraft

Will the Navy have enough ASW-capable ships and aircraft between now and 2010? Should recently deactivated ASW-capable ships and aircraft be returned to service? The Navy in recent years has deactivated a substantial number of ASW-capable ships and aircraft, including Spruance (DD-963) class destroyers, Oliver Hazard Perry (FFG-7) class frigates, TAGOS-type ocean surveillance ships, carrier-based S-3 airplanes, and land-based P-3 maritime patrol aircraft. Since ASW traditionally has been a platform-intensive undertaking — meaning that a significant number of platforms (e.g., ships and aircraft) traditionally has been required to conduct an effective ASW operation against a small number of enemy submarines, or even a single submarine — some observers have expressed concern about the resulting decline in numbers of U.S. Navy ASW-capable platforms.[149]

As discussed in the Background section, the Navy plans to shift to a new, less platform-intensive ASW concept of operations. The Navy also plans to introduce new ASW-capable platforms in coming years, including Littoral Combat Ships (LCSs). The Navy's proposal for a 313-ship fleet includes 55 LCSs. Fully realizing the new ASW concept of operations, however, may take some time, particularly in light of the technical challenges involved, and LCSs will not be available in large numbers until after 2010. This raises a potential question of whether the Navy will have enough ASW-capable ships and aircraft between now and 2010, and whether the Navy should reactivate recently retired ASW-capable platforms and keep them in service until the new ASW concept is substantially implemented and larger numbers of LCSs and other new ASW-capable platforms join the fleet.

Advocates of this option could argue that the recent retirements of ASW-capable platforms occurred before the dimensions of the PLA Navy submarine modernization effort were fully understood. Opponents could argue that even with these recent retirements, the Navy retains a substantial number of such platforms, including SSNs, Aegis cruisers and destroyers, remaining Oliver Hazard Perry (FFG7) class frigates, carrier- and surface combatant-based SH-60 helicopters, and remaining P-3s. They could also argue that there are more cost-effective ways to improve the Navy's ASW capabilities between now and 2010, such as increased ASW training and exercises (see discussion below).

NAVY WARFARE AREAS AND PROGRAMS

Missile Defense

Replacement for NAD Program

Is the Missile Defense Agency's sea-based terminal missile defense program sufficiently robust?

In December 2001, DOD announced that it had canceled the Navy Area Defense (NAD) program, the program that was being pursued as the Sea-Based Terminal portion of the Administration's overall missile-defense effort. (The NAD program was also sometimes called the Navy Lower Tier program.) In announcing its decision, DOD cited poor performance, significant cost overruns, and substantial development delays.

The NAD system was to have been deployed on Navy Aegis cruisers and destroyers. It was designed to intercept short- and medium-range theater ballistic missiles in the final, or descent, phase of flight, so as to provide local-area defense of U.S. ships and friendly forces, ports, airfields, and other critical assets ashore. The program involved modifying both the Aegis ships' radar capabilities and the Standard SM-2 Block IV air-defense missile fired by Aegis ships. The missile, as modified, was called the Block IVA version. The system was designed to intercept descending missiles within the Earth's atmosphere (endoatmospheric intercept) and destroy them with the Block IVA missile's blast-fragmentation warhead.

Following cancellation of the program, DOD officials stated that the requirement for a sea-based terminal system remained intact. This led some observers to believe that a replacement for the NAD program might be initiated. In May 2002, however, DOD announced that instead of starting a replacement program, MDA had instead decided on a two-part strategy to (1) modify the Standard SM-3 missile — the missile to be used in the sea-based midcourse (i.e., Upper Tier) program — to intercept ballistic missiles at somewhat lower altitudes, and (2) modify the SM-2 Block four air defense missile (i.e., a missile designed to shoot down aircraft and cruise missiles) to cover some of the remaining portion of the sea-based terminal defense requirement. DOD officials said the two modified missiles could together provide much (but not all) of the capability that was to have been provided by the NAD program. One aim of the modification strategy, DOD officials suggested, was to avoid the added costs to the missile defense program of starting a replacement sea-based terminal defense program.

The Missile Defense Agency's (MDA's) FY2008 budget submission for the Aegis BMD program now divides the sea-based terminal program into a near-term (Block 2008) capability and a far-term (Block 2014) capability. The Block 2008 capability includes a fuze-modified SM-2 Block IV and is to provide a near-term sea-based terminal capability against a finite set of SRBMs. The Navy (not MDA) is funding the modification of 100 SM-2 Block IV missiles. This capability is scheduled to enter service in FY2009. MDA states that the Block 2014 capability is envisioned as including a new type of missile, the design of which is not yet determined, that is to provide a more capable and robust sea-based terminal capability. Reported options for the new missile include a system using a modified version of the Army's Patriot Advanced Capability-3 (PAC-3) interceptor or a modified version of the Navy's new Standard Missile 6 Extended Range Active Missile (SM-6 ERAM) air defense missile.[150]

In light of PLA TBM modernization efforts, including the possibility of TBMs equipped with MaRVs capable of hitting moving ships at sea, one potential issue is whether the sea-based terminal program as outlined in MDA's FY2008 budget submission is sufficiently robust in terms of schedule and annual funding levels.

Ships with CG(X) Radar Capabilities

Should planned annual procurement rates for ships with CG(X) radar capabilities be increased?

The Navy is planning to procure a new kind of cruiser called the CG(X) as the replacement for its 22 remaining Ticonderoga (CG-47) class Aegis cruisers. Navy plans call for the CG(X) to be equipped with a new radar that, compared to the Aegis system's SPY-1 radar, is more powerful and thus more capable for supporting ballistic missile defense operations. If improvements to Aegis radar capabilities are not sufficient to achieve the Navy's desired radar capability for countering modernized PLA TBMs, then CG(X) radar capabilities could become important to achieving this desired capability.

As part of its FY2006-FY2011 Future Years Defense Plan (FYDP) submitted to Congress in February 2005, the Navy accelerated the planned start of CG(X) procurement from FY2018 to FY2011. The Navy wants to procure 19 CG(X)s between FY2011 and FY2023. If procured on that schedule, the ships might enter service between 2017 and 2029.[151]

In light of PLA TBM modernization efforts, including the possibility of TBMs equipped with MaRVs capable of hitting moving ships at sea, one issue is whether it would be feasible to accelerate planned CG(X) procurement. Given the time needed to develop the CG(X)'s new radar, it might not be possible to accelerate the procurement of the first CG(X) from FY2011 to an earlier year.

Once CG(X) procurement were to begin however, it might be possible to accelerate the procurement dates of later ships in the program, so as to get more of the ships in service sooner. Issues to address for this option would include industry capacity and available financial resources. Based on past procurement rates for Aegis cruisers and destroyers, industry capacity might not pose a significant constraint to accelerated CG(X) procurement. In light of the CG(X)'s potential procurement cost, accelerating procurement of CG(X)s to earlier years would, in a situation of a constrained Navy budget, leave less funding available in those years for meeting other Navy needs.

A second potential issue concerns the potential affordability of the CG(X) design. In a situation of a constrained Navy budget, the procurement cost of the CG(X) combined with funding demands for other Navy needs might make it difficult for the Navy to complete a 19-ship CG(X) procurement program by FY2023. If so, then one potential alternative would be to design a reduced-cost alternative to the CG(X) that preserves CG(X) radar capabilities while reducing other CG(X) payload elements. Such a ship might be more easily procured in desired numbers within available resources. The option of a reduced-cost alternative to the CG(X) that preserves certain CG(X) capabilities while reducing others is discussed in more detail in another CRS report.[152]

Number of SM-3 Missiles Planned for Procurement

Is the number of SM-3 interceptors that DOD plans to procure sufficient?

The Standard Missile 3 (SM-3) is the Navy's ballistic missile defense interceptor. DOD is currently planning to procure a total of 147 SM-3s. One potential oversight issue for Congress is whether this planned total is sufficient in light of potential numbers of Chinese TBMs to be countered. A May 2007 press report stated that:

> A preliminary DOD study points to the need for more Standard Missile-3 (SM-3) sea-based missile defense interceptors and Terminal High-Altitude Area Defense (THAAD) interceptors, according to Lt. Gen. Kevin Campbell, commander of U.S. Army Space and Missile Defense Command (SMDC).

The study examined various major combat operations around the world, estimating the percentages of enemy missiles that would be taken out by conventional forces or felled by system failures. The current SM-3/THAAD interceptor inventory then was compared to a list of critical assets identified by DOD combatant commanders that need to be defended.

Near-term U.S. missile defense capabilities are "limited" primarily by interceptor inventory, Campbell said at a May 16 breakfast in Washington sponsored by National Defense University. In addition to SM-3s and THAAD interceptors, DOD also needs more Patriot battalions and ground-based interceptors, according to Campbell.[153]

AIR WARFARE

Mix of F/A-18E/Fs and F-35 Joint Strike Fighters (JSFs)

Should the Navy's planned mix of carrier-based F/A-18E/F strike fighters and F-35 Joint Strike Fighters (JSFs) be changed to include more JSFs and fewer F/A-18E/Fs?

The Department of the Navy, which includes the Navy and the Marine Corps, plans to procure a mix of F/A-18E/F Super Hornet strike fighters and F-35 Joint Strike Fighters (JSFs). The F/A-18E/Fs would be operated by the Navy, and the JSFs would be operated by both services. Marine Corps JSFs could be operated from Navy carriers to perform Navy missions. The F/A-18E/F incorporates a few stealth features and is believed to be very capable in air-to-air combat. Compared to the F/A-18E/F, the JSF is much more stealthy and is believed to be more capable in air-to-air combat.

The growing number of fourth-generation fighters and strike-fighters in the PLA Air Force and the PLA Naval Air Force, and the growing number of modern PLA SAM systems, raises a potential question of whether the Navy should change its planned mix of carrier-based strike fighters to include more Navy JSFs and fewer F/A-18E/Fs. Such a change would produce a force with a better ability to avoid PLA SAM systems and more total air-to-air combat capability than the currently planned force.

The Department of the Navy's planned mix of F/A-18E/Fs and JSFs can be compared to the Air Force's strike fighter procurement plans. The Air Force plans to replace its current force of F-15 and F-16 fighters with a mix of F-22 Raptor strike fighters and JSFs. The F-22 is more stealthy and capable in air-to-air combat than the JSF. The Navy does not have an equivalent to the F-22. The Air Force argues that a mix of F-22s and JSFs will be needed in the future in part to counter fourth-generation fighters and strike fighters operated by other countries, including China. Supporters of the F-22 argue that the challenge posed by fourth-generation fighters in combination with modern integrated air defenses, is a key reason for procuring 381 or more F-22s, rather than the planed number of 179.[154] Potential oversight questions include the following:

- If the Air Force is correct in its belief that a combination of F-22s and JSFs will be needed in part to counter fourth-generation fighters and modern SAM systems operated by other countries, including China, would the Department of the Navy's planned mix of JSFs and F/A-18E/Fs be sufficient to counter a PLA force of fighters and strike fighters that includes fourth-generation designs?
- If PLA attacks on U.S. air bases in the Western Pacific reduce the number of Air Force F-22s and JSFs that can participate in a conflict in the Taiwan Strait area, would the Department of the Navy's planned mix of F/A-18E/Fs and JSFs have sufficient air-to-air combat capability to counter the PLA's force of fighters and strike fighters?[155]

Anti-Air Warfare (AAW)

Surface Ship AAW Upgrades

Are current Navy plans for upgrading surface ship anti-air warfare (AAW) capabilities adequate?

The PLA's acquisition of advanced and highly capable ASCMs such as the SSN-27 Sizzler and the SS-N-22 Sunburn raises the question of whether current plans for modernizing Navy surface ship AAWcapabilities are adequate. The Government Accountability Office (GAO) in previous years has expressed concerns regarding the Navy's ability to counter ASCMs.[156] Potential areas for modernization include, among other things, the following:

- ship radars, such as the SPY-1 radar on Aegis ships or the radars now planned for the DDG-1000 destroyer and CG(X) cruiser;
- AAW-related computer networking capabilities, such as the Cooperative Engagement Capability (CEC) and the Naval Integrated Fire Control-Counter Air (NIFC-CA) system;[157]

- air defense missiles such as the Standard Missile,[158] the Evolved Sea Sparrow Missile (ESSM), and the Rolling Airframe Missile (RAM);
- close-in weapon systems, such as the Phalanx radar-directed gun;
- potential directed-energy weapons, such as solid state or free-electron lasers;
- decoys, such as the U.S.-Australian Nulka active electronic decoy; and
- aerial targets for AAW tests and exercises, particularly targets for emulating supersonic ASCMs.[159]

Littoral Combat Ship (LCS) AAW Capability

Should the currently planned AAW capability of the Littoral Combat Ship (LCS) be increased?

The Navy's Littoral Combat Ship (LCS) is to be armed with 11 Rolling Airframe Missiles (RAMs). The ship will also be equipped with an AAW decoy launcher.[160]

The PLA's acquisition of ASCMs that can be fired from aircraft, surface ships, and submarines raises the possibility that LCSs participating in a conflict in the Taiwan Strait area could come under attack by substantial numbers of ASCMs. Other Navy ships, such as Aegis cruisers and destroyers and, in the future, DDG1000 destroyers and CG(X)s cruisers, could help defend LCSs against attacking ASCMs, but such ships might not always be in the best position to do this, particularly if ASCMs are launched at LCSs from undetected submarines or if the supporting U.S. Navy ships are busy performing other duties. If LCSs were damaged or sunk by ASCMs, the Navy's ability to counter enemy mines, submarines, and small boats — the LCS's three primary missions — would be reduced.

The possibility that the LCS's AAW system might be overwhelmed or exhausted by attacks from multiple ASCMs raises the question of whether the AAW capability planned for the LCS should be increased. Options for increasing the LCS's planned AAW capability include, among other things, adding another 11round RAM launcher or supplementing the currently planned RAM launcher with a battery of Evolved Sea Sparrow (ESSM) missiles. In assessing such options, one factor to consider would be whether installing additional RAMs or ESSMs would require an increase in the planned size and cost of the LCS.

Antisubmarine Warfare (ASW)

Technologies

Are current Navy efforts for improving antisubmarine warfare (ASW) technologies adequate?

In addition to the issue discussed earlier of whether the Navy between now and 2010 will have enough ASW-capable platforms, another potential issue raised by the PLA submarine modernization effort is whether current Navy plans for improving antisubmarine warfare (ASW) technologies are adequate. The Navy states that it intends to introduce several new ASW technologies, including distributed sensors, unmanned vehicles, and technologies for networking ASW systems and platforms. In March 2007, Admiral Mullen testified that:

Submarines with improving stealth and attack capability — particularly modern diesel attack submarines — are proliferating world-wide at an alarming rate. Locating these relatively inexpensive but extremely quiet boats presents our Navy with a formidable challenge. Navy is pursuing a distributed and netted approach to ASW. Some of the key ASW programs we must continue to develop and field as quickly as possible include: the Deployable Distributed Autonomous system (DADS); the Reliable Acoustic Path Vertical Line Array (RAPVLA); the Surface Ship Torpedo Defense System (SSTD); the Aircraft Carrier Periscope Detection Radar (CVNPDR); and, the High Altitude ASW Weapon Concept (HAAWC)....

The Navy continues to pursue research and development of Distributed Netted Sensors (DNS); low-cost, rapidly deployable, autonomous sensors that can be fielded in sufficient numbers to provide the cueing and detection of adversary submarines far from the Sea Base. Examples of our FY 2008 request of $24 million in these technologies include:

- Reliable Acoustic Path, Vertical Line Array (RAP VLA). A passive-only distributed system exploiting the deep water propagation phenomena. In essence, a towed array vertically suspended in the water column.
- Deep Water Active Distributed System (DWADS). An active sonar distributed system optimized for use in deep water.
- Deployable Autonomous Distributed System (DADS). A shallow water array, using both acoustic and non-acoustic sensors to detect passing submarines. DADS will test at sea in FY 2008.

- Littoral ASW Multi-static Project (LAMP). A shallow water distributed buoy system employing the advanced principles of multi-static (many receivers, one/few active sources) sonar propagation.

Further developing the Undersea Warfare Decision Support System (USW-DSS) will leverage existing data-links, networks, and sensor data from air, surface, and sub-surface platforms and integrate them into a common ASW operating picture with tactical decision aids to better plan, conduct, and coordinate ASW operations. We are requesting $23 million in FY 2008 towards this system.

To engage the threat, our forces must have the means to attack effectively the first time, every time. The Navy has continued a robust weapons development investment plan including $293 million requested in the FY 2008 on such capabilities as:

- High-Altitude ASW Weapons Concept (HAAWC). Current maritime patrol aircraft must descend to very low altitude to place ASW weapons on target, often losing communications with the sonobuoy (or distributed sensor) field. This allows the aircraft to remain at high altitude and conduct an effective attack while simultaneously enabling the crew to maintain and exploit the full sensor field in the process. This capability will be particularly important in concert with the new jet-powered P-8A MMA. A test is scheduled for May 2007.
- Common Very Lightweight Torpedo (CVLWT). The Navy is developing a 6.75" torpedo suitable for use in the surface ship and submarine antitorpedo torpedo defense, and the offensive Compact Rapid Attack Weapon (CRAW) intended for the developing manned and unmanned aerial vehicles.... Platform Sensor Improvements. Against the quieter, modern diesel-electric submarines, work continues on both towed arrays and hull mounted sonars. Our $410 million request in FY 2008 includes work on the following:
- TB-33 thin-line towed array upgrades to forward deployed SSN's provides near term improvement in submarine towed array reliability over existing TB-29 arrays. TB-33 upgrades are being accelerated to Guam based SSN's.
- Continued development of twin-line thin line (TLTL) and vector-sensor towed arrays (VSTA) are under development for mid-far term capability gaps. TLTL enables longer detection ranges/contact holding times, improves localization, and classification of contacts. VSTA is an Office of Naval Research project that would provide

TLTL capability on a single array while still obviating the bearing ambiguity issue inherent in traditional single line arrays.[161]

Training and Exercises

Are current Navy plans for ASW training and exercises adequate?

As mentioned earlier, success in an ASW operation is highly dependent on the proficiency of the people operating the ASW equipment, and ASW operational proficiency can take time to develop and can atrophy significantly if not regularly exercised. At various times since the end of the Cold War, some observers have expressed concerns about whether the Navy was placing adequate emphasis on maintaining ASW proficiency. The Navy in April 2004 established a new Fleet ASW Command, based in San Diego, to provide more focus to its ASW efforts, and since then has taken steps to enhance its ASW training and exercises:

- In April 2004, it was reported that carrier strike groups deploying from the U.S. West Coast would now stop in Hawaiian waters for three- to five-day ASW exercises before proceeding to the Western Pacific.[162]
- In March 2005, the Navy reached an agreement to lease a Swedish non-nuclear-powered submarine and its crew for a 12-month period. The submarine, which is equipped with an air-independent propulsion (AIP) system, arrived in San Diego in June 2005, where it is being used to as a mock enemy submarine in Pacific Fleet ASW exercises.[163]
- The Navy in 2005 also reached an agreement with Colombia and Peru under which one non-nuclear-powered submarine from each country deployed to the Navy base at Mayport, FL, in April 2005 to support Atlantic Fleet ASW exercises for a period of two to five months. South American non-nuclear-powered submarines have been integrated into U.S. Navy exercises since 2002.[164]
- In October 2005, the commander of the Navy's Pacific Fleet said that, upon assuming command earlier in the year, he made ASW his highest priority and instituted a cyclic approach to ASW training that includes more frequent (quarterly) assessments, as well as training exercises with other navies.[165]

In light of these actions, the potential question is whether the Navy ASW training and exercises are now adequate, or whether they should be expanded further.

Active-Kill Torpedo Defense

If feasible, should Navy plans for acquiring an active-kill torpedo defense system be accelerated?

Navy surface ships and submarines are equipped with decoy systems for diverting enemy torpedoes away from their intended targets. Such decoys, however, might not always work, particularly against wake-homing torpedoes, which can be difficult to decoy. Under the Navy's surface ship torpedo defense (SSTD) development program, the U.S. Navy is developing an "active-kill" torpedo-defense capability for surface ships and also submarines that would use a small (6.75-inch diameter) anti-torpedo torpedo (ATT) to physically destroy incoming torpedoes. In March 2007, Admiral Michael Mullen, the Chief of Naval Operations, testified that the Navy's surface ship torpedo defense (SSTD) program

> delivers near term and far term torpedo defense. The planned FY 2008 $16 million R and D [research and development] investment supports ongoing development of the 6 ¾ inch Common Very Lightweight Torpedo (CVLWT) which supports both the Anti-Torpedo Torpedo (ATT) and the Compact Rapid Attack Weapon (CRAW). Also, several capability upgrades to the AN/SLQ-25A (NIXIE) [torpedo decoy system] are being incorporated to improve both acoustic and nonacoustic system performance to counter current threat torpedoes. These enhancements also support their use in the littorals and are scheduled to complete in FY 2009. The AN/WSQ-11 System uses active and passive acoustic sensors for an improved torpedo Detection Classification and Localization (DCL) capability, and a hard kill Anti-Torpedo Torpedo (ATT) to produce an effective, automated and layered system to counter future torpedo threats. DCL improvements include lower false alarm rates and better range determination.[166]

In light of the modern torpedoes, including wake-homing torpedoes, that are expected to be carried by modern PLA submarines, a potential question is whether, if feasible, the current ATT acquisition schedule should be accelerated.

Mine Warfare

Are current Navy mine warfare plans adequate?

The PLA's interest in modern mines may underscore the importance of the Navy's efforts to develop and acquire new mine countermeasures (MCM) systems, and perhaps raise a question regarding whether they should be expanded or accelerated. The Navy's MCM capabilities have been a matter of concern among members of the congressional defense committees for several years.

Conversely, the PLA Navy's own reported vulnerability to mines (see section on PLA Navy limitations and weaknesses) can raise a question regarding the less-frequently-discussed topic of the U.S. Navy's offensive mine warfare capability. To what degree can minelaying complicate PLA plans for winning a conflict, particularly a short-duration conflict, in the Taiwan Strait area? Do U.S. Navy plans include sufficient mines and minelaying platforms to fully exploit the PLA Navy's vulnerability to mines? The Navy has various mines either in service or under development.[167]

Computer Network Security

Are Navy efforts to ensure computer network security adequate?

The PLA's published interest in IW/IO, and concerns that recent attacks on U.S. computer networks have in some cases originated in China, underscore the importance of U.S. military computer network security. The Navy in July 2002 established the Naval Network Warfare Command in part to prevent and respond to attacks on Navy computer networks.[168] Another CRS report discusses computer network security at length.[169]

Emp Hardening

Are Navy efforts to harden its systems against electromagnetic pulse (EMP) adequate?

The possibility that the PLA might use nuclear weapons or high-power microwave (HPM) weapons to generate electromagnetic pulse (EMP) effects against the electronic systems on U.S. Navy ships and aircraft raises a potential question regarding the adequacy of the Navy's efforts to harden its systems against EMP effects. A 2004 commission studying the EMP issue expressed concerns about the potential vulnerability of U.S. tactical forces to EMP.[170]

The commission's report was received at a July 22, 2004, hearing before the House Armed Services Committee. At the hearing, Representative Steve Israel asked about the role of EMP in exercises simulating operations in the Taiwan Strait:

Representative Steve Israel: [Representative Roscoe] Bartlett and I just attended an NDU [National Defense University] tabletop [exercise] with respect to the Straits of the Taiwan just last week. To your knowledge, has there been any tabletop exercise, has there been any simulation, any war-game that anticipates an EMP attack, and, if there has not been, do you believe that that would, in fact, be a useful exercise for NDU, the Pentagon or any other relevant entity? Dr. Graham, do you want to answer that?

Dr. William R. Graham (Commission Chairman): Thank you. Let me poll the commission and see if they have any experience with that. General Lawson?

General Richard L. Lawson, USAF (Ret.) (Commissioner): No, sir.

Graham: Dr. Wood?

Dr. Lowell L. Wood, Jr. (Commissioner): I don't believe there's been any formal exercise, certainly not to my knowledge. There's been extensive discussion of what the impact of Chinese EMP laydowns would be, not on Taiwan, which is, after all, considered by China to be part of its own territory, but on U.S. forces in the region which might be involved in the active defense of Taiwan. In particular, the consequences the EMP laydown on U.S. carrier task forces has been explored, and while, it's not appropriate to discuss the details in an open session like this, the assessed consequences of such an attack, a single-explosion attack, are very somber.

Since that is a circumstance in which the target might be considered a pure military one in which the loss of life might be relatively small, but the loss of military capability might be absolutely staggering, it poses a very attractive option, at least for consideration on the part of the Chinese military.

I would also remark that Chinese nuclear explosive workers at their very cloistered research center in northwestern China very recently published an authoritative digest and technical commentary on EMP in English, in a Chinese publication. It is very difficult to understand what the purpose of publishing a lengthy, authoritative article in English in a Chinese publication would be, if it was not to convey a very pointed message. This came not from military workers. It came from the people who would be fielding the weapon that would conduct the attack.

Graham: Dr. Pry on our staff has made a survey of foreign writings on EMP, and he noted that while U.S. exercises have not to our knowledge played that scenario, Chinese military writings have discussed that scenario. So it's certainly something they have thought of and it is within their mind. I have observed generally over the last 40 years that there's a tendency in the U.S. military not to introduce nuclear weapons in general and EMP in particular into exercise scenarios or game scenarios because it tends to end the game, and that's not a good sign. I think it would be a very interesting subject for the NDU group to take up and see and force them not to end the game. Time will not stop if such an event happens. Let them understand what the consequences will be.[171]

Later in the hearing, Representative Roscoe Bartlett returned to the topic of the potential effects of EMP on Navy ships:

> Representative Bartlett: If China were to detonate a weapon high over our carrier task force, can we note in this [open] session what would the effects on the carrier task force be?
>
> Graham: Mr. Bartlett, several years ago, the Navy dismantled the one simulator it had for exposing ships directly [to EMP]. It was the Empress simulator located in the Chesapeake Bay. So I don't believe any direct experimental work has been done for quite some time.
>
> However, the general character of modern naval forces follows the other trends we've described, which is an increasing dependence upon sophisticated electronics for its functionality, and, therefore, I believe there's substantial reason to be concerned.
>
> [Would] Any other commissioners [care to comment]?
>
> Representative Bartlett: Dr. Wood?
>
> Wood: In open session, sir, I don't believe it's appropriate to go much further than the comment that I made to [Representative] Israel that the assessments that are made of such attacks and their impacts are very somber.
>
> The Navy generally believes — that portion of the Navy that's at all cognizant of these matters — that because they operate in an extremely radar-intensive environment, [since] they have a great deal of electromagnetic gear on board, some of which radiates pulses — radar pulses, for instance — because they can operate in that type of environment, that they surely must be EMP robust. These free-floating beliefs on the part of some Navy officers are not — repeat not — well grounded technically.[172]

Chapter 4

LEGISLATIVE ACTIVITY FOR FY2008

FY2008 DEFENSE AUTHORIZATION BILL (H.R. 1585)

House

Section 1244 of the House-reported version of the FY2008 defense authorization bill (H.R. 1585) states:

SEC. 1244. SENSE OF CONGRESS CONCERNING THE STRATEGIC MILITARY CAPABILITIES AND INTENTIONS OF THE PEOPLE'S REPUBLIC OF CHINA.

It is the sense of Congress that —

(1) United States military war-fighting capabilities are potentially threatened by the strategic military capabilities and intentions of the People's Republic of China, as demonstrated by —
(A) the October 2006 undetected broach of a Chinese SONG-class diesel-electric submarine in close proximity of the USS Kitty Hawk in international waters; and
(B) the January 2007 test of a direct ascent anti-satellite (ASAT) weapon, posing a potential threat to United States military assets in space;

(2) it is in the national security interests of the United States to make every effort to understand China's strategic military capabilities and intentions; and

(3) as part of such an effort, the Secretary of Defense should expand efforts to develop an accurate assessment of China's strategic military modernization, particularly with regard to its sea- and space-based strategic capabilities.

Appendix

ADDITIONAL DETAILS ON CHINA'S NAVAL MODERNIZATION EFFORTS [173]

This appendix presents additional details and commentary on several of the elements of China's military modernization discussed in the Background section of this book.

THEATER-RANGE BALLISTIC MISSILES (TBMs)

Regarding the potential for using TBMs against moving U.S. Navy ships at sea, ONI states that "One of the newest innovations in TBM weapons developments involves the use of ballistic missiles to target ships at sea. This is assessed as being very difficult because it involves much more than just a missile."[174] ONI continues:

> The use of ballistic missiles against ships at sea has been discussed for years. Chinese writings state China intends to develop the capability to attack ships, including carrier strike groups, in the waters around Taiwan using conventional theater ballistic missiles (TBMs) as part of a combined-arms campaign. The current conventional TBM force in China consists of CSS-6 and CSS-7 short-range ballistic missiles (SRBMs) deployed in large numbers. The current TBM force would be modified by changing some of the current missiles' ballistic reentry vehicles (RVs) to maneuvering reentry vehicles (MaRVs) with radar or IR seekers to provide the accuracy needed to attack ships at sea. The TBMs with MaRVs would have good defense penetration capabilities because of their high reentry speed and maneuverability. Their lethality could be increased, especially with terminally guided submunitions.

In order to attack a ship or a carrier battle group with TBMs, the target must be tracked, and its position, direction, and speed determined. This information would be relayed in near real time to the missile launchers. China may be planning ultimately to use over-the-horizon (OTH) radar, satellites, and unmanned aerial vehicles (UAVs) to monitor the target's position. Reconnaissance assets would be used to detect the ship or carrier strike group before it entered into the range of Chinese TBMs, facilitating early preparation for the engagement, and refining the target's position. Target information would be relayed through communication satellites or other channels to a command center, and then to the missile launchers. TBMs with MaRVs would then be launched at the target's projected position. The missiles would fly their preplanned trajectories until onboard seekers could acquire the ship and guide the missiles to impact.[175]

Another observer states:

The PLA's historic penchant for secrecy and surprise, when combined with known programs to develop highly advanced technologies that will lead to new and advanced weapons, leads to the conclusion that the PLA is seeking [to] field new weapon systems that could shock an adversary and accelerate their defeat. In the mid-1990s former leader Jiang Zemin re-popularized an ancient Chinese term for such weapons, "Shashaojian," translated most frequently as "Assassin's Mace," or "silver bullet" weapons.

One potential Shashoujian is identified by the [DOD's 2005 report on China military power]: a maneuvering ballistic missile design to target U.S. naval forces. In 1996 a Chinese technician revealed that a "terminal guidance system" that would confer very high accuracy was being developed for the DF-21 [intercontinental ballistic missile, or ICBM]. Such a system could employ a radar similar to the defunct U.S. Pershing-2 MRBM or could employ off-board sensors with rapid data-links to the missile tied to satellite-navigation systems. Nevertheless, should such missiles be realized they will pose a considerable threat as the U.S. Navy is not yet ready to deploy adequate missile defenses.[176]

A separate observer states:

Land-based conventional tipped ballistic missiles with maneuverable (MarV) warheads that can hit ships at sea.... would be a Chinese "assassin's mace" sort of capability — something impossible to deal with today, and very difficult under any circumstances if one is forced to defend by shooting down ballistic missiles. The capability is dependent on Beijing's ability to put together the appropriate space-based surveillance, command, and targeting architecture necessary to make this work.[177]

One more observer states:

> There is yet another exceedingly important chapter being written in the [PLA] ballistic-missile saga. China is trying to move rapidly in developing ballistic missiles that could hit ships at sea at MRBM [medium-range ballistic missile] ranges — in other words, to threaten carriers beyond the range at which they could engage Chinese forces or strike China. Among its other advantages for China, this method of attack avoids altogether the daunting prospect of having to cope with the U.S. Navy submarine force — as anti-submarine warfare is a big Chinese weakness. Along with these efforts to develop ballistic missiles to hit ships, they are, of course, working diligently to perfect the means to locate and target our carrier strike groups (CSGs). In that regard, an imperfect or rudimentary (fishing boats with satellite phones) means of location and targeting might be employed even earlier than the delay of several more years likely needed to perfect more reliable and consistent targeting of ships. Chinese missile specialists are writing openly and convincingly of MaRV'd ballistic missiles (missiles with maneuverable reentry vehicles) that maneuver both to defeat defenses and to follow the commands of seekers that spot the target ships. There seems little doubt that our naval forces will face this threat long before the Taiwan issue is resolved.[178]

LAND-ATTACK CRUISE MISSILE (LACMs)

Regarding LACMs, ONI states:

> Land-attack cruise missiles (LACMs) are available for sale from many countries, and are marketed at arms shows around the world. Land-attack cruise missiles are becoming a significant adjunct to theater ballistic missiles in strike and deterrent roles. The number of countries manufacturing and purchasing LACMs continues to grow. Some of the systems in development are derivatives of antiship missiles, and some are dedicated designs, and a few weaponized UAVs [unmanned aerial vehicles] complete the inventory....
> Israel, China, Germany, and South Africa are among the countries with LACM development programs.[179]

Another observer states:

> Taiwanese civilian and military officials contend that in 2005 the PLA has started deployment of its long-awaited new land attack cruise missiles (LACMs).32 Asian sources contend that two Chinese companies are making LACMs; one for the Second Artillery missile forces, and one for PLA Navy and

PLA Airforce platforms, most likely based on the new 300+ km range YJ-62 anti-ship missile.33 It has been well reported that China has sought to develop modern LACMs since the 1970s and has sought technology from Russia, Israel, and has obtained at least six Russian Novator Kh-55 LACMs via the Ukraine, and has obtained parts of U.S. RGM/UGM-109 Tomahawk LACMs via Iraq, Afghanistan and very likely, Pakistan. When these LACMs are married to new Russian-assisted EO and Radar satellites, French assisted communication satellite, access to U.S., Russian and European navigation satellites signals, and then carried by Russian assisted nuclear submarines or future Russian-made bombers, then the PLA will have its first limited non-nuclear global strike capability.34 Such a synergy could emerge by 2010 or shortly thereafter. This might not equal the U.S. all-weather intimate moving-target hitting capability, but China may be able to use LACMs for political-military influence much as the U.S. does today.[180]

ANTI-SHIP CRUISE MISSILES (ASCMs)

Regarding the SS-N-27s carried by the eight newly delivered Kilo-class submarines, ONI states:

> Russia continues to develop supersonic ASCMs. The most interesting is the 3M-54E design which has a cruise vehicle that ejects a rocket-propelled terminal sprint vehicle approximately 10 nautical miles from its target. The sprint vehicle accelerates to speeds as high as Mach 3 and has the potential to perform very high-g defensive maneuvers.[181]

Another observer states that "the very dangerous and lethal SS-N-27Bs [are] said by experts to be part of the best family of ASCMs in the world...."[182]

LAND-BASED SURFACE-TO-AIR MISSILES (SAMs)

Regarding SAM systems, DOD states:

> In the next few years, China will receive its first battalion of Russian-made S-300PMU-2 surface-to-air missile systems. With an advertised intercept range of 200 km, the S-300PMU-2 provides increased lethality against tactical ballistic missiles and more effective electronic countermeasures. China also is developing the indigenous HQ-9 air defense missile system, a phased array radar-based SAM with a 150 km range.[183]

Additional Details on China's Naval Modernization Efforts

Another observer states:

One area where Russian technology in particular is producing a new and dangerous PLA capability is that of modern air defenses. The PLA Air Force is on its way to purchasing up to 14 to 20 Battalions of Russian S-300/PMU-1/PMU-2 surface-to-air missiles (SAMs), which could mean the purchase of 700 to 1,000 of these deadly missiles. The S-300 family is very difficult to jam and can only be evaded with some assurance by stealthy F-22A or B-2 aircraft. The range of the S-300PMU-2 allows it to target aircraft that operate over Taiwan, thus denying the Taiwan Strait as an air defense buffer zone for the Taiwan Air Force. Jane's reports that China may be funding the development of the even longer-range S-400 missile, while Asian sources report that China may be co-producing the deadly short range TOR-M1,44 which can shoot down precision-guided cruise missiles and bombs.[184]

LAND-BASED AIRCRAFT

Regarding land-based aircraft, DOD states:

China has more than 700 combat aircraft based within an un-refueled operational range of Taiwan and the airfield capacity to expand that number significantly. Many aircraft in the PLA force structure are upgrades of older models (e.g., re-engined B-6 bombers for extended ranges); however, newer aircraft make up a growing percentage of the inventory.

— The PLA Air Force (PLAAF) is deploying the F-10 multi-role fighter to operational units. The F 10, a fourth generation aircraft, will be China's premier fighter in the coming decades.
— China is now producing the multi-role Su-27SMK/FLANKER (F-11A) fighter under a licensed co-production agreement with Russia following an initial production run of Su-27SKs (F-11). China is employing increasing numbers of the multi-role Su-30MKK/FLANKER fighter-bomber and its naval variant, the Su-30MK2.
— Chinese aircraft are armed with an increasingly sophisticated array of air-to-air and air-to-surface weapons, satellite and laser-guided precision munitions, and cruise missiles....

- Improvements to the FB-7 fighter program will enable this older aircraft to perform nighttime maritime strike operations and use improved weapons such as the Kh-31P (AS-17) anti-radiation missile and KAB-500 laser-guided munitions.[185]

DOD also states that:

PLA air defense has shifted from point defense of key military, industrial, and political targets to a new Joint Anti-Air Raid Campaign based on a modern, integrated air defense system and offensive and defensive counter-air operations. These operations extend beyond the defense of Chinese airspace to include strikes against an adversary's bases (including aircraft carriers) and logistics to degrade the adversary's ability to conduct air operations.

The air defense component of anti-access/area-denial includes SAMs such as the SA-10, SA-20, HQ-9, HQ-15, and extended-range C2 suites such as the S-300PMU2. Beijing will also use Russian-built and domestic fourth-generation aircraft (e.g., Su-27 and Su-30 FLANKER variants, and the indigenous F-10). The PLA Navy would employ recently acquired Russian Su-30MK2 fighters, armed with AS-17/Kh-31A anti-ship missiles. The acquisition of refueling aircraft, including the Russian IL-78/MIDAS and the indigenously developed B-6U refueling aircraft, will extend operational ranges for PLAAF and PLA Navy strike aircraft armed with precision munitions, thereby increasing the threat to surface and air forces distant from China's coast. Additionally, acquisition of UAVs and UCAVs, including the Israeli HARPY, expands China's options for long-range reconnaissance and strike.[186]

ONI states:

China operates a force of 1950s vintage B-6D Badger dedicated naval strike bombers. Today, these aircraft are armed with the C601, an air-launched derivative of the Styx ASCM, but a program to arm them with the modern C802K is underway....

China and Russia also are working on new tactical aircraft dedicated to the antiship mission. China's FB-7 Flounder has been in development since the 1970s; its production limited by engine difficulties. The C801K-armed FB-7 entered service with the Chinese Navy, and integration of the longer-range C802K on the FB-7 is underway.[187]

Another observer states:

> Although the modernization of the PLA Air Force has taken a backseat to nuclear, space, and naval development, the PLAAF is a much more modern fighting force in 2007 than it was in 1997. It now boasts about 450 advanced fighter aircraft, including about 300 Russian-designed fourth-generation Su-27 Flankers and Chinese Jian-11s and 76 Su-30MKK fighter-bombers, which display substantial ground attack capabilities and are armed with Russia's most advanced air-to-air missiles.
>
> In January 2007, the PLAAF unveiled its new Jian-10 multirole fighter jet, which is based on the Israeli Lavi airframe, itself an evolutionary offshoot of the F-16. As of March 2007, the PLAAF had reportedly deployed 60 Jian-10s, with the total production run estimated at around 250. Although its forward-wing canards are a novelty among Chinese-designed fighters, the Jian-10's most remarkable characteristic is its midair refueling module. The PLAAF has been practicing in-flight refueling since at least 2005 with both Su-27 and older Jian-8 fighters. Following Peace Mission 2005, a joint Chinese — Russian military exercise on China's Shandong peninsula, China contracted for six to 10 Illyushin-78s configured as aerial refueling platforms and 30 Illyushin-76 cargo aircraft configured for paratroop drops.
>
> The increasing size of China's fourth-generation fighter fleet, which is heavily armed with the latest Russian and Chinese air-to-air missiles and equipped with fire control systems and refueling modules, gives the PLAAF a technological and numerical edge in the Taiwan Strait.[188]

SUBMARINES

Regarding China's submarine force, one observer states that by 2010,

> the PLA Navy could take delivery of over 20 new domestic SONG A and YUAN-class conventional submarines, 12 Russian KILO-877/636/636M conventional submarines, and five or more new indigenous Type 093 nuclear attack submarines (SSNs) — the third Type 093 is now under construction. In addition, the PLAN could retain up to 20 older Type 035 MING-class conventional [attack submarines] and about 4 older Type 091 HAN-class SSNs. This raises the prospect by 2010 of a Chinese fleet of over 50 modern-tomoderate [sic] attack submarines capable of engaging Taiwan, U.S. and Japanese naval forces.[189]

Another observer states that:

> the PLA Navy now has the capability to make the antisubmarine warfare (ASW) mission very difficult for U.S. forces. With a total of more than 50 operational submarines, and with a substantial number of them new and quiet, China, quite simply, can put to sea more submarines than the U.S. Navy can locate and counter. Its older Ming and Romeo submarines are not only still lethal if ignored but also serve to disperse and dilute the efforts of the ASW forces. In other words, some, or even many, of the already large and diverse, but still rapidly growing, fleet of very capable Shang SSNs, and Kilo, Song, and Yuan SSs can reasonably expect to remain undetected as they seek to interdict the U.S. carrier strike groups. If the "shooting has started," eventually U.S. ASW forces could take a big toll against the Chinese submarine force, but the delay in sanitizing the area before the entry of carrier strike groups is what the Chinese are counting on as adequate delay to present the world with the aforementioned *fait accompli* with respect to Taiwan.[190]

Another observer states:

> Evidence suggests that China is seeking to become a first-class submarine power. While the PLAN modernization shows impressive breadth with major new purchases of naval aircraft and surface combatants, submarines appear to be the centerpiece of China's strategic reorientation toward the sea. The May 2002 contract for eight additional Kilos, the likely continuation of the Song program, and nuclear force modernization, taken together with the evident new priority on training, technological research and doctrinal development all suggest that Beijing recognizes the value of submarines as a potent, asymmetric answer to United States maritime superiority. The recent ascendance of a submariner, Adm. Zhang Dingfa, to the position of commanding officer of the PLAN underlines these tendencies. Further investments in diesel submarines, particularly when enhanced by air independent propulsion, will afford Beijing increasing near-term leverage in the East Asian littoral, while methodical nuclear modernization signifies a long-term commitment to global power projection. As one Chinese strategist recently observed, "The scale [of recent purchases] indicates that in the coming years, China will build an offshore defense system with submarines as the key point."[191]

The paragraphs below discuss China's submarine modernization effort in more detail on a class-by-class basis.

Jin-Class (Type 094) SSBN

China is building a new class of SSBN known as the Jin class or Type 094. The first two Jin-class boats are expected to enter service in 2008 and 2010. Additional units are expected, perhaps at two-year intervals. A total of four to six boats are expected.[192] The Jin-class design may be derived from the Shang-class (Type 093) SSN design discussed below. ONI states that China "wishes to develop a credible, survivable, sea-based deterrent with the capability to reach the United States" and that the Jin-class design "benefits from substantial Russian technical assistance."[193]

The Jin-class SSBN is expected to be armed with 12 JL-2 nuclear-armed submarine-launched ballistic missiles, also known as JL-2s. DOD estimates that these missiles will enter service between 2007 and 2010, and that they will have a range of 8,000+ kilometers (about 4,320+ nautical miles).[194] Such a range could permit Jin-class SSBNs operating in protected bastions close to China to attack targets in Hawaii, Alaska, and locations in the continental United States that are north and west and north of a line running from central or southern California to northern Minnesota.[195] A March 2007 news article states:

> China's military is engaged in a major buildup of submarines that includes five new strategic nuclear-missile boats and several advanced nuclear-powered attack submarines, according to the Office of Naval Intelligence.
>
> The new nuclear-powered missile submarines (SSBNs), identified as Type 094s, will be outfitted with new 5,000-mile range JL-2 missiles that "will provide China with a modern and robust sea-based nuclear deterrent force," the ONI stated in report made up of written answers to questions on the Chinese submarine buildup.
>
> The ONI report was first disclosed to *Sea Power* magazine, and a copy was obtained by *The Washington Times*. It was the first time the Pentagon has identified the number of new Chinese strategic submarines under construction.
>
> The five new missile submarines will "provide more redundancy and capacity for a near-continuous at-sea SSBN presence," the ONI said, which noted that sea trials for some of the submarines are under way and the first deployments could begin as early as next year.[196]

Shang-Class (Type 093) SSN

China is building a new class of SSN, called the Shang (or Type 093) class. DOD states that the first Shang-class SSN began sea trials in 2005.[197] Construction of a third may have begun, but has not yet been confirmed. A total of five boats is expected.

Observers believe the Shang-class SSNs will likely represent a substantial improvement over China's five older and reportedly fairly noisy Han (Type 091) class SSNs, which entered service between 1974 and 1990. The first Han-class boat reportedly was decommissioned in 2003, and observers expect the others will be decommissioned as Shang-class boats enter service.

The Shang class reportedly was designed in conjunction with Russian experts and is derived from the Soviet Victor III-class SSN design that was first deployed by the Soviet Union around 1978. The Victor III was the first in a series of quieter Soviet SSN designs that, by the mid-1980s, led to substantial concern among U.S. Navy officials that the Soviet Union was closing the U.S. lead in SSN technology and thereby creating what Navy officials described an antisubmarine warfare (ASW) "crisis" for the U.S. Navy.[198]

ONI states that the Shang-class "is intended primarily for antisurface warfare at greater ranges from the Chinese coast than the current diesel force. China looks at SSNs as a primary weapon against aircraft carrier battle groups and their associated logistics support."[199] Observers expect the Shang-class boats to be armed with a modern ASCM and also with a LACM broadly similar to the U.S. Tomahawk land-attack cruise missile. One observer states:

> At first, [China's LACMs] will be launched by Second Artillery units, but soon after, they may also be used by PLA Air Force H-6 bombers and by the Navy's new Type 093 nuclear attack submarines. When used by the latter, the PLA will have its first platform capable of limited but politically useful non-nuclear power projection on a global scale....
>
> Once there is a build-up of Type 093s it should be expected that the PLA Navy may undertake patrols near the U.S. in order to draw U.S. SSNs back to defensive patrols.[200]

Regarding the Jin- and Shang-class programs, one set of observers state:

> Whereas the Yuan's debut allegedly surprised Western analysts, the emergence of China's [Type] 093 SSN and [Type] 094 SSBN has been anticipated for some time. Nevertheless, these programs remain shrouded in mystery, and there is little consensus regarding their operational and strategic

significance. In the broadest terms, it can be said that a successful [Type] 093 program will significantly enlarge the scope of Chinese submarine operations, perhaps ultimately serving as the cornerstone of a genuine blue-water navy. The [Type] 094 could take the survivability of China's nuclear deterrent to a new level, potentially enabling more aggressive posturing by Beijing in a crisis. Moreover, these platforms are entering the PLA Navy (PLAN) at a time when reductions are projected to occur in the U.S. Navy submarine force; that fact was duly noted by a senior PLAN strategist recently in one of China's premier naval journals.[201]

These observers also state:

Chinese sources universally recognize that noise reduction is one of the greatest challenges in building an effective nuclear submarine. PRC scientists have long been conducting research concerning the fundamental sources of propeller noise. For instance, experts at China Ship Scientific Research Center developed a relatively advanced guide-vane propeller by the late 1990s. This, and the fact that China already has advanced seven-blade propellers with cruciform vortex dissipaters on its indigenous Song-class and imported Kilo-class diesel submarines, suggests that the [Type] 093 and [Type] 094 will have significantly improved propellers. A researcher in Qingdao's 4808 Factory also demonstrates Chinese attention to the need to use sound-isolation couplings to prevent transmission of vibrations to the ocean from major fresh-water circulating pumps in the steam cycle. Advanced composite materials are credited with capability to absorb vibrations and sound.

One Chinese researcher states that the [Type] 093 is not as quiet as the U.S. Seawolf class or Virginia class but is on a par with the improved Los Angeles class. Another analyst estimates that the [Type] 093's noise level has been reduced to that of the Russian Akula-class submarine at 110 decibels. He states that the [Type] 094's acoustic signature has been reduced to 120 decibels. According to this report, this is definitely not equal to that of the Ohio class, but is on a par with the Los Angeles. There is no additional information given to evaluate concerning the origins or comparability of these "data."[202]

Kilo-Class SS

China ordered four Kilo-class SSs from Russia in 1993; the ships entered service in 1995-1999. The first two were of the less capable (but still fairly capable) Project 877 variant, which Russia has exported to several countries; the other two were of the more capable Project 636 variant that Russia had previously reserved for its own use.

China in 2002 ordered eight additional Kilos from Russia, reportedly all of the Project 636 design. Five of the boats were reportedly delivered in 2005, and the remaining three reportedly were delivered in 2006.[203] ONI states that the delivery of these eight boats "will provide the Chinese Navy with a significant qualitative increase in warfighting capability,"[204] while another observer states that the Kilo-class boats are "Among the most worrisome of China's foreign acquisitions....."[205]

The eight Kilos are believed to be armed with wire-guided and wake-homing torpedoes, and with the Russian-made SS-N-27 Sizzler ASCM, also known as the Novator Alfa Klub 3M-54E — a highly capable ASCM that might as difficult to shoot down, or perhaps even more difficult to shoot down, than the SS-N-22 Sunburn ASCM on China's Russian-made Sovremenny-class destroyers (see discussion below on surface combatants). The four Kilos commissioned in 1995-1999 are expected to be refitted in Russia; upgrades are expected to include installation of the SS-N-27 ASCM.

Yuan-Class (Type 041) SS

China is building a new class of SS called the Yuan (or Type 041) class. The first Yuan-class boat, whose appearance reportedly came as a surprise to western observers,[206] was launched (i.e., put into the water for the final stage of construction) in 2004. Observers expect the first Yuan-class boat to enter service in 2006 and the second to enter service in 2008.

Some observers believe the Yuan class may incorporate technology from Russia's most recent SS design, known as the Lada or Amur class, including possibly an air-independent propulsion (AIP) system.[207] One observer says the Yuan class strongly resembles both the Russian Amur 1650-class and French Agosta-class SS designs.[208] Another set of observers states:

> Evidence of China's advances in submarine design and construction emerged in July 2004, when Western media reports suddenly revealed China's production of the new Yuan class of conventional submarine. While much is still unknown about the Yuan, it appears to possess attributes of both the Song- and Kilo-class vessels, suggesting that China may have optimized features from each vessel class to meet its specific requirements for underwater warfare.[209]

Song-Class (Type 039/039G) SS

China is also building a relatively new SS design called the Song (or Type 039/039G) class. The first Song-class boat entered service in 1999, and a total of 13 are expected to be in service by 2006. It is unclear whether there will be any additional boats beyond the 13th.

The first boat reportedly experienced problems, resulting in design changes that were incorporated into subsequent (Type 039G) boats. Some observers believe the Song-class design may have benefitted from PLA Navy experience with the Kilo class. One report states that one Song-class boat has been equipped with an AIP system.[210] One set of observers states:

> The design and production rates of China's new Song-class diesel submarine represent a significant advance over its predecessor, the Ming-class submarine. The Song class has a hydrodynamically sleek (teardrop) profile, possesses new cylindrical environmental sensors, and relies on German engines for propulsion. Most significantly, the Song is much quieter because it is fitted with an asymmetrical seven-blade skew propeller, and the Song uses anechoic

Older Ming-Class (Type 035) and Romeo-Class (Type 033) SSs

China in 2005 also had about 20 older Ming (Type 035) class SSs and about 16 even-older Romeo (Type 033) class SSs.

The first Ming-class boat entered service in 1971 and the 20th was launched in 2002. Production may have ended in favor of Song- and Yuan-class production. In April 2003, a malfunction aboard one of the boats (hull number 361) killed its 70man crew. Observers believe they were killed by carbon monoxide or chlorine poisoning. The boat was repaired and returned to service in 2004.

China's Romeo-class boats entered service between the early 1960s and the late 1980s. A total of 84 were built. Of the 16 still in service as of 2006, one is a modified boat that has been used as a cruise missile test ship. Ten additional Romeos that until recently were in reserve status (and of dubious operational condition) reportedly have all been scrapped. The total number of Romeos in service has been declining over time.

If China decides that Ming- and Romeo-class boats have continued value as minelayers or as bait or decoy submarines that can be used to draw out enemy submarines (such as U.S. SSNs), it may elect to keep some of these older submarines in service even as new submarines enter service.

Aircraft Carriers

Regarding China's activities for developing an aircraft carrier, one observer stated in May 2007 that:

> For over a year, the PLAN has been more or less open about China's eventual deployment of an aircraft carrier battle group. Except for the carrier, China has all the elements of a carrier battle group in place, according to Lieutenant General Wang Zhiyuan of the PLA General Armaments Department. China will finish constructing its first aircraft carrier by 2010, according to an unnamed lieutenant general (probably General Wang again), but its first operational carrier will likely be the Varyag, the former Soviet carrier bought from Ukraine.
>
> China's once-secret naval aviation program appears to be underway at full steam. At its center is the massive 67,000-ton former Ukrainian aircraft carrier, which the Chinese government extracted from the Black Sea in 2001 after considerable costs in both treasure and political capital with Turkey. In March 2002, the Varyag finally completed its 15,200-mile journey to its new home port of Dalian, where it was immediately placed under heavy security at the PLAN dry docks.
>
> China has reportedly negotiated a contract for 48 Sukhoi-33 jet fighters, the carrier-based version of the Su-27, and is now preparing the Varyag's flight deck for flight operations. Reports in the PRC media indicate that China will also configure its new Jian-10 fighter for carrier operations.
>
> The PLAN Air Force (PLANAF) schedule apparently envisions developing a carrier air wing by the time China launches its own aircraft carrier, despite official Beijing's continuing protestations that while "China already is capable of building an aircraft carrier, a final decision on construction has not yet been made."[212]

Another observer states:

> The [Chinese] aircraft carrier conundrum resurfaced in mid-[2005] when the former Russian carrier Varyag, which had arrived at [the Chinese port of] Dalian on 4th March 2002, emerged from dock painted in Chinese naval colours. This led to speculation, intensified by the construction of two new Type 051C Louzhou class destroyers in the same dockyard, that deployment of the ship was imminent. Wide discussion of its potential roles included development into a fully operational carrier or amphibious ship or a more modest function as an aviation training vessel (the name Shi Lang has been suggested). In the event, the ship did not go to sea in 2005 and lack of information continues to frustrate objective assessment. In particular, the material state of Varyag when it arrived in China is unclear. The outward appearance of the ship suggested that she had not been well

maintained and that possibly she was derelict. If this was the case, there would be a requirement for a very large work-package including the checking and/or replacement of wiring, installation of electronic systems, setting to work of main machinery, which did not appear to have been removed before transfer, and raising habitability to acceptable standards. All of this could be achieved, at a cost, but it would probably require longer than the ten weeks spent by the ship in dock during 2005.[213]

Another observer states:

The year 2005 marked a turning point in China's willingness to continue to deny or obfuscate its ambitions to build aircraft carriers. Last May it moved the old Russian uncompleted aircraft carrier hulk the Varyag, that it purchased and moved to Dalian harbor in 2002, from dockside into a drydock. It then emerged in early August painted in PLA Navy grey, and the most recent Internet-source photos show that the carrier deck is receiving new multiple coatings. China's ruse was that the Varyag would be turned into a casino and Chinese officials have repeatedly denied they were developing carriers. But on March 10, Hong Kong's Wen Wei Po quoted General Wang Zhiyuan, a Deputy Director of the Science and Technology Committee of the General Armaments Department, that in "three to five years," "The Chinese army will conduct research and build an aircraft carrier and develop our own aircraft carrier fleet." He went on to add that the escort and support ships for this carrier group are either being built or have already been built. These would likely include the new Luyang 1, Luyang 2 and Luzhou class air defense destroyers launched from 2003 to 2005, new Type 093 nuclear powered attack submarines, and new Fuchi class underway replenishment ships.

If General Wang is to be believed, then the carrier Varyag, now undergoing what appears to be substantial refurbishment, will be used for some kind of military mission. These could include the refinement of China's anti-aircraft carrier doctrine and tactics, training and development of a new carrier air wing, and future aerial and amphibious support combat missions. In August 2005 Russian sources interviewed at the Moscow Airshow offered confirmation of China's carrier plans in that two Russian companies offered that China was interested in two types of future carrier combat aircraft, the Sukhoi Su-33 and the Chengdu J-10 modified with a new Russian engine thrust vector to enable slower carrier landing speeds. The Russians also used the Moscow Airshow to market the twin-seat Su-33UB, but modified with thrust vector engines. It is quite likely that all three will be upgraded with new more powerful Russian Al-31 engines, have new active-phased array radar, and carry a range of active guided and helmet display sighted air-to-air missiles and precision ground attack missiles. As such both could offer some performance parameters that equal or even exceed that of the U.S. Boeing F/A-18E/F, the main U.S. carrier combat aircraft. Internet sources also indicate that China is developing a carrier-sized AWACS aircraft that could also be developed into antisubmarine and cargo support variants. While the U.S. Navy benefits from its over 70 years of constant practice and employment of effective carrier aviation, it is nonetheless a major shock that China's carrier fleet could commence with combat capabilities that could neutralize those of the U.S. Navy in some scenarios.[214]

A press report states:

> Chinese shipyard workers have been repairing a badly damaged ex-Russian aircraft carrier and have repainted it with the country's military markings, raising the question once again of whether China is pursuing longer-term plans to field its first carrier.
> In the latest developments, images show that workers at the Chinese Dalian Shipyard have repainted the ex-Russian Kuznetsov-class aircraft carrier Varyag with the markings and colour scheme of the People's Liberation Army (PLA) Navy (PLAN). Additional new photographs show that other work, the specifics of which could not be determined, appears to be continuing and that the condition of the vessel is being improved....
> Still, China's ultimate intentions for the Varyag remain unclear. One possibility is that Beijing intends to eventually have it enter into some level of service. A military strategist from a Chinese military university has commented publicly that the Varyag "would be China's first aircraft carrier."
> It is possible that the PLAN will modify the Varyag into a training aircraft carrier. A US intelligence official said the vessel could be made seaworthy again with enough time, effort and resources. However, US defence officials said that repairing the Varyag to become fully operational would be an extraordinarily large task. The carrier was about 70 per cent complete at the time of transfer and sensitive portions were destroyed, including damage to the core structure, before China was permitted to take possession. Given the difficulty and expense, it is questionable whether Beijing would pursue the effort only to use the Varyag as a training platform; such a move could, however, mark a transitional phase en route to a fully operational capability.
> Another possibility is that China does, indeed, plan to repair the vessel to become its first seagoing aircraft carrier or use knowledge gained from it for an indigenously built carrier programme. The US intelligence official said such an outcome "is certainly a possibility" if China is seeking a blue-water navy capable of protecting long-range national interests far from its shores such as sea lanes in the Strait of Malacca. If this strategy were to be followed, China would have to reinstate the structural integrity degraded before delivery and study the structural design of the carrier's deck. These two activities, along with the blueprints and the ship itself, could be used to design an indigenous carrier. Such a plan would

Additional Details on China's Naval Modernization Efforts

very likely be a long-term project preceded by the development of smaller vessels such as amphibious landing ships.[215]

Another set of observers states that China's increased shipbuilding capacity

has direct implications for China's ability to build an aircraft carrier. For the past decade, rumors have circulated that China is interested in buying or building a carrier. A Chinese military delegation is known to have considered buying Ukraine's Varyag, and the Spanish shipbuilder Bazan is reported to have submitted to China a design for a basic carrier.... China now has eight yards capable of VLCC and ULCC[216] construction, and it will add more such yards in the coming years. Many of these yards would be suitable for the construction of a large carrier. Another option for China would be to build a medium-sized carrier (30,-50,000 tons) for launching and retrieving helicopters or vertical short take-off/landing (VSTOL) fixed-wing aircraft. Such a ship could be built from a relatively basic design based on LHD-type platforms (i.e., multipurpose amphibious assault ships) similar to the ones used by the United Kingdom, Japan, and Thailand. Such a vessel could also be completed at a number of modern yards in China, even ones without VLCC capacity — although with substantial naval shipbuilding experience.

Although Chinese shipbuilders are quite capable of building the hull, other parts of China's defense industry would have to develop the equipment necessary to outfit an aircraft carrier with the necessary propulsion systems, navigational electronics, or weapon suites for self-defense or long-range operations. In addition, China lacks the capability to build either large-capacity aircraft-lift elevators or steam catapults for the movement and launching of aircraft; so a Chinese carrier would have to rely on a ski-jump design. Thus, a Chinese carrier would not resemble in any way, shape, or form a U.S. "big-deck" carrier, which serves as the operational hub for an entire carrier battle group. If China chooses to build an aircraft carrier, the need for more ships will become especially pressing in order to regularly protect and replenish the carrier. The PLAN currently lacks enough modern, multipurpose warships to adequately meet the needs of defending and replenishing a carrier. It is to this end that an expanding and improving shipbuilding infrastructure is a necessary condition for the development of modern, long-range naval capabilities.[217]

Surface Combatants

One observer states that by 2010, China's surface combatant force

could exceed 31 destroyers and 50 frigates, backed up by 30 ocean-capable stealthy fast attack craft. Such a force could then be used in conjunction with submarines and attack aircraft to impose a naval blockade around Taiwan.

Surface ships could also defend the airspace around Taiwan from U.S. Naval forces, especially its P-3 anti-submarine warfare aircraft which would play a critical role in defeating a blockade.[218]

Another set of observers states that improvements in China's shipbuilding industry

> are also reflected in the improvements in Chinese warships commissioned in the late 1990s and in many of the new naval projects currently coming online. The newest vessels are more durable, are more capable of surviving damage, have longer ranges, are stealthier, and are capable of carrying a variety of modern weapon systems. China's serial production of a variety of new naval platforms in the past five years is notable in this regard. The current degree of simultaneous production of several new classes of naval platforms has not been seen in China for decades.[219]

Luhai (Type 051b) Destroyer

One set of observers states:

> The Luhai-class destroyer, which was launched in October 1997 and commissioned into the PLAN in late 1998, represented a significant design advance over China's second-generation Luhu-class destroyer. In terms of overall size, the Luhai is 20 percent larger. It has a widened hull beam to enhance stability, armament-carrying capacity, and crew living space. In particular, the Luhai's larger size permits four quad launchers for C801/C802 anti-ship missiles, which is double the number, deployed on the Luhu. The Luhai also uses a gas turbine engine, which is more powerful than the Luhu's diesel gas turbine system. In addition, the design of the Luhai's bridge and superstructure exhibits a number of stealthy characteristics (particularly in comparison to the Luhu's structure). These design features include a streamlined superstructure with inclined angles and two solid masts with fewer protruding electronic sensor arrays. The stepped superstructure may have been designed with the intention to equip the Luhai with vertical launch systems, possibly for SAMs for an enhanced area-defense capability. The absence of such a system on the Luhai suggests that that option was deferred for a time.[220]

Luyang I (Type 052 B) and II (Type 052C) Destroyers

One set of observers states that the Luyang I and II classes

> represent important advances in the shipbuilding industry's overall design and production techniques.... The latter have a similar design as the former, but they appear to be optimized for air-defense missions....

These four new destroyers represent an important evolution in shipbuilding design capabilities, production techniques, and management practices. The hulls are larger than the Luhai's, which increases their weapons capacity, versatility, and stability on the high seas. The designs of these vessels are even stealthier, with sloped sides and a superstructure with a reduced profile — attributes that, collectively, reduce the vessel's radar signature. Also, these hulls were built using modular shipbuilding, a technique increasingly widespread in China's most modern shipyards. Modular construction (as opposed to keel-up) allows for work to be done on different sections at the same time, increasing the efficiency and speed of the production process. One of the most significant aspects of the new destroyers is the fact that China constructed these four new destroyers at the same time and quite quickly as well, at least compared with past experiences. This serial production of an indigenously designed vessel is a first in the PRC's naval history and a testament to improved project management. The four new 052B- and 052C-class vessels have been built or have been under construction within the past four years. By comparison, in the entire decade of the 1990s China only built a second Luhu (1993) and one Luhai (1997) destroyer.

The 052C-class destroyer, in particular, possesses several important attributes. First, according to Goldstein and Murray, it uses a phased array or planar radar on the four corners of the bridges' vertical superstructure, which would be used with a SAM vertical launch system (VLS) for air-defense missiles — a second important innovation. Both of these attributes are a first for a Chinese combatant and help the PLAN resolve its long-standing weakness with air defense. In the past, Chinese combatants relied on short-range SAMs for air defense. A medium-range VLS SAM system would provide the Chinese navy with its first, real area-defense vessel, and a collection of such ships could allow the PLA Navy to operate surface action groups. If China is able to successfully reverse engineer Russian-purchased SAMs, then it may deploy them on the 052C destroyer. Some reports indicate that China may deploy its HQ-9 system (a Chinese version of a Russian SAM with a range of about 120 km) on the new destroyers. Such a system on the front of the new platform, combined with older Chinese SAMs in the stern, would give the Chinese their first fleet air-defense vessels.[221]

Regarding the radar to be carried by the Luyang II class, a January 2006 press article states: "The two Chinese Project 052C destroyers have fixed array radars that are often described as active arrays, though that cannot be certain."[222] Active radar arrays use a technology that is more modern and more capable in certain respects than the technology used in the SPY-1 radars on the U.S. Navy's Aegis ships.

Regarding the HQ-9 SAM believed to be carried by the Luyang II-class destroyers, ONI states:

> The most challenging threat to aircraft and cruise missiles comes from high-performance, long-range [SAM] systems like the Russian SA-10/SA-20 family. The system combines very powerful three-dimensional radar and a high-performance missile with engagement ranges in excess of 100 nautical miles against a conventional target. The SA-10/SA-20 has been marketed widely and has enjoyed some success in the export market, but its high cost has limited its proliferation. Technology from the SA-10 is being incorporated into China's 50-nautical mile range HQ-9 SAM, which is intended for use on the new LUYANG destroyer. The HQ-9 will provide China's navy with its first true area air defense capability when the SAM becomes operational in the next few 223 years.

Jiangkai (Type 054) Frigates

One set of observers states that the Jiangkaiclass design

> is larger and more modern than that of China's Jiangwei II — class frigates. Like China's new destroyers, the new frigate has a more streamlined design and has a larger displacement. These changes augment the new vessel's warfighting capabilities and its seaworthiness. Some sources note that the 054 frigate resembles the French Layfayette-class guided-missile frigate because of the minimalist design of the Type 054's superstructure. The design of the new frigate also offers greater options for outfitting the vessel with various weapon suites. Some estimates indicate that the new frigate will have a significantly enhanced set of weapon capabilities over the Jiangwei-class frigates, possibly including VLS capabilities.[224][4]

Amphibious Ships

The three new classes of amphibious ships and craft now under construction in China, all of which began construction in 2003, are as follows:

- Yuting II-class helicopter-capable tank landing ships (LSTs).
- Three of these ships entered service in 2003 and another six in 2004.
- Each ship can transport 10 tanks and 250 soldiers, and has a helicopter landing platform for two medium-sized helicopters. The ships were built at three shipyards, and two more are reportedly under construction.
- Yunshu-class landing ships (LSMs). Ten of these ships entered service in 2004. Each ship can transport 6 tanks or 12 trucks or 250 tons of supplies. The ships were built at four shipyards, and observers believe additional units might be built.
- Yubei-class utility landing craft (LCUs). Eight of these landing craft entered service in 2004 and another two in 2005. Each craft can transport 10 tanks and 150 soldiers. The ships were built at four shipyards, and observers expect additional units.

DOD states:

The PLA has increased amphibious ship production to address its lift deficiencies; however, the Intelligence Community believes these increases alone will be inadequate to meet requirements. The PLA is also organizing its civilian merchant fleet and militia, which, given adequate notification, could augment organic lift in amphibious operations. Transport increases were accompanied by an increase of 25,000 troops, 200 tanks and 2,300 artillery pieces in the military regions opposite Taiwan, according to the latest figures from DIA. The increased troops and equipment in these military regions all appear capable of participating in expeditionary operations.[225]

Another observer states:

On December 20, 2006, China launched the PLAN's largest combat amphibious assault ship, an indigenously designed amphibious landing dock (LPD) identified as the Type 071, which is similar to but a little bigger than the U.S. Whidbey Island-class LPD.[226] Designed in the 10th five-year plan (2001 — 2005), the ship was built in about six months in the second half of 2006 and appears to be the first of four LPDs. The Type 071 appears to be designed to land 500 — 800 troops and 25 — 50 armored vehicles and supplies using 15 landing craft or several large hovercraft. It will carry at least two Changhe Z-8 helicopters, each capable of transporting 30 soldiers inland beyond the beachhead.[227]

Another set of observers states that

> China's development and production of new classes of amphibious vessels [is] a testament to the SBI's [shipbuilding industry's] improved production capacity, as well as to advances in ship-design and project-management skills. In the past few years, China has designed a new class of landing ships/tanks (LSTs) and has built at least seven of them. This new follow-on to the Yuting-class vessels is enlarged and has a greater carrying capacity. With these new ships, China's inventory of LSTs has grown from 16 to 23. China also designed and built several new medium-landing ships (LSMs), which appear to be a follow-on to China's Yuedeng-class vessels. In addition, Goldstein and Murray note that the PLA Navy aspires to building a 12,300-ton amphibious transport dock (LDP) capable of transporting several helicopters and air-cushion landing crafts.[228]

Information Warfare/Information Operations (IW/IO)

Regarding IW/IO capabilities, ONI states, without reference to any specific country:

> IO is the combination of computer network attack, electronic warfare, denial and
> deception (D and D), and psychological operations (PSYOP)....
> Outside attack on Navy networks can take different forms depending on the attacker's goals and sophistication. Navy networks have been targeted for denial of service attacks from the Internet. More sophisticated operations, perhaps conducted by foreign military or intelligence services, might include covertly mapping Navy networks, installing backdoors to facilitate future intrusions, stealing data, and leaving behind destructive code packages to be activated in time of conflict. Malicious codes like the Melissa virus have appeared in classified networks, demonstrating that an external attack on ostensibly protected networks could succeed. Attacks could selectively alter information in Navy databases and files, introducing errors into the system. When discovered or revealed, this corruption of trusted data could cause us to lose confidence in the integrity of the entire database.[229]

Additional Details on China's Naval Modernization Efforts

A November 2006 press report stated that:

> Chinese computer hackers penetrated the Naval War College network earlier this month, forcing security authorities to shut down all e-mail and official computer network work at the Navy's school for senior officers.
>
> Navy officials said the computer attack was detected Nov. 15 and two days later the U.S. Strategic Command raised the security alert level for the Pentagon's 12,000 computer networks and 5 million computers.
>
> A spokesman for the Navy Cyber Defense Operations Command, located in Norfolk, said "network intrusions" were detected at the Newport, R.I., military school two weeks ago.
>
> "The system-network connection was terminated and known affected systems were removed and are being examined for forensic evidence to determine the extent of the intrusion," said Lt. Cmdr. Doug Gabos, the spokesman.
>
> "The Naval War College computer system-network is used by students at the war college and contains Navy Professional Reading Program and other materials, all of which are unclassified information."...
>
> Cmdr. Gabos declined to comment on the origin of the attack. "The nature and extent of intrusion are operational issues," he said. "I can tell you it was an isolated incident and did not affect other elements of Department of Defense."
>
> However, the U.S. Strategic Command, which is in charge of Defense Department computer warfare and defenses, issued a directive about the time the attack was detected ordering all defense computer users to heighten security by changing passwords....
>
> Alan Paller, a computer security specialist with the private SANS Institute, said the Chinese network attack against the war college is "the tip of the iceberg."
>
> "The depth of the penetration is more than anybody is even admitting," he said in an interview. "People are trying to hide this because they're embarrassed."
>
> Mr. Paller said the Chinese military's doctrine calls for waging cyber-warfare against computer networks. "Part of it is gathering data and part is leaving a back door so they can get in [to military computers] in the future," he said.[230]

Commenting on this event, another observer states:

> In mid-November [2006], computer security officials determined that Chinese hackers had penetrated the computer network at the Naval War College in Rhode Island. Retired Air Force Major General Richard Goetze, a professor at the Naval War College, said the Chinese took down the entire Naval War College

computer network, an operation that prompted the U.S. Strategic Command to raise the security alert level for the Pentagon's 12,000 computer networks and 5 million computers. One report hinted that the Chinese cyberwarriors may have been targeting the college's Strategic Studies Group, which had begun developing concepts for waging cyberwarfare.[231]

Nuclear Weapons

Regarding the potential use of nuclear weapons against U.S. Navy forces, one study states that

> there is some evidence the PLA considers nuclear weapons to be a useful element of an anti-access strategy. In addition to the nuclear-capable [ballistic] missiles... China has nuclear bombs and aircraft to carry them, and is reported to have nuclear mines for use at sea and nuclear anti-ship missiles. At the very least, China would expect the presence of these weapons and the threat to use them to be a significant deterrent to American action.[232]

Regarding the possibility of China using a high-altitude nuclear detonation to create an EMP effect, DOD states:

> Some PLA theorists are aware of the electromagnetic effects of using a high-altitude nuclear burst to generate high-altitude electromagnetic pulse (HEMP), and might consider using HEMP as an unconventional attack, believing the United States and other nations would not interpret it as a use of force and as crossing the nuclear threshold. This capability would most likely be used as part of a larger campaign to intimidate, if not decapitate, the Taiwan leadership. HEMP causes a substantial change in the ionization of the upper atmosphere, including the ionosphere and magnetosphere. These effects likely would result in the degradation of important war fighting capabilities, such as key communication links, radar transmissions, and the full spectrum of electro-optic sensors. Additional effects could include severe disruptions to civil electric/power and transportation. These effects cannot easily be localized to Taiwan and would likely affect the mainland, Japan, the Philippines, and commercial shipping and air routes in the region.[233]

Whether China would agree with the above view that EMP effects could not easily be localized to Taiwan and surrounding waters is not clear. The effective radius of a high-altitude EMP burst is dependent to a strong degree on the altitude at which the warhead is exploded (the higher the altitude, the greater the radius).[234] China might therefore believe that it could detonate a nuclear warhead somewhere east of Taiwan at a relatively low altitude, so that the resulting EMP radius would be sufficient to affect systems in Taiwan and on surface ships in surrounding waters, but not great enough to reach systems on China's mainland.[235] Following the detonation,

China could attempt to confuse the issue in the public arena of whose nuclear warhead had detonated. Alternatively, China could claim that the missile launch was an accident, and that China command-detonated the warhead at altitude as a failsafe measure, to prevent it from detonating closer to the surface and destroying any nearby ships.[236]

High-Power Microwave (HPM) Weapons

Regarding radio-frequency weapons, DOD states:

> Chinese technicians are working to develop several types of "new concept" weapon systems, two of which are radio frequency and laser-based systems.
>
> Long-range beam weapons would use narrow radio frequency (RF) beams to engage targets such as aircraft or precision guided munitions (PGMs). Short-range systems would be packaged into missiles or artillery shells and launched into the vicinity of targets such as radars or command posts before releasing an RF pulse. In recent years, the application of RF weapons has expanded to include deployment on small vehicles or in suitcases for targeting critical military or civilian infrastructures where close access is possible.
>
> PRC officials have publicly indicated their intent to acquire RF weapons as a means of defeating technologically advanced military forces. Chinese writings have suggested that RF weapons could be used against C4ISR, guided missiles, computer networks, electronically-fused mines, aircraft carrier battle groups, and satellites in orbit.
>
> Analysis of Chinese technical literature indicates a major effort is underway to develop the technologies required for RF weapons, including high-power radiofrequency sources, prime-power generators, and antennas to radiate RF pulses.[237]

ONI states:

> Radio-frequency weapons (RFW) could be used against military networks since they transmit high power radio/microwave energy to damage/disrupt electronic components. RFWs fall into two categories, beam and warhead. A beam weapon is a multiple use system that can repeatedly send directional RF energy at different targets. An RF warhead is a single-use explosive device that can be delivered to the target by multiple means, including missiles or artillery shells. RFWs can be assembled with little technical knowledge from commercial off-the-shelf components, such as surplus military radars.[238]

One observer states that, "at least one U.S. source indicates the PLA has developed" non-nuclear radio frequency warheads for ballistic missiles.[239] When asked at a hearing about the possibility of China using a nuclear weapon to generate an EMP effect against Taiwan and U.S. naval forces, this observer stated:

> What worries me more, Congressman, is non-nuclear electromagnetic pulse weapons. Non-nuclear explosive propelled radio frequency or EMP-like devices that could be used with far greater frequency and far more effect because they would not run the danger for China of prompting a possible nuclear response. Thereby it would be much more tempting to use and use effectively.
>
> If you could combine a non-nuclear radio frequency weapon with a maneuvering ballistic missile of the type that the Pentagon report describes very briefly this year, that would constitute a real Assassin's Mace weapon. One that, in my opinion, we cannot defend ourselves against and would possibly effectively deny effective military — effective American military intervention in the event of — not just a Taiwan crisis, but other crises as well.[240]

REFERENCES

[1] John M. Donnelly, "China On Course To Be Pentagon's Next Worry," *CQ Weekly*, May 2, 2005, p. 1126.

[2] Donald C. Winter, "Navy Transformation: A Stable, Long-Term View," *Heritage Lectures*, No. 1004, March 19, 2007, [remarks] delivered February 7, 2007, p. 2. (Published by The Heritage Foundation)

[3] Dave Ahearn, "Mullen Says Military Faces Financial Crisis, But Nation Can Afford Arms," *Defense Daily*, April 5, 2007. The passage as originally published was in the form of five one-sentence paragraphs and has been condensed here into two paragraphs for ease of reading.

[4] "Interesting Times," *Defense Daily*, May 7, 2007.

[5] U.S. Department of Defense, *Annual Report To Congress [on] Military Power of the People's Republic of China, 2007*. Washington, Office of the Secretary of Defense, released May 25, 2007. (Hereafter cited as *2007 DOD CMP*.) Previous annual editions cited similarly.

[6] U.S. Department of the Navy, *Worldwide Maritime Challenges 2004*, Washington, prepared by the Office of Naval Intelligence. (Hereafter cited as *2004 ONI WMC*.)

[7] The white papers are entitled *China's National Defense in 2006* and *China's National Defense in 2004*. (Hereafter cited as *2006 China White Paper* and *2004 China White Paper*.) The English-language texts of the papers can be found on the Internet at [http://www.fas.org/nuke/guide/china/ doctrine/ wp 2006.html] and [http://www.fas.org/ nuke/guide/china/ doctrine/natdef 2004. html].

[8] Transcript hereafter cited as *7/27/05 HASC hearing*.

[9] Hereafter cited as *3/16/06 USCC hearing* and *9/15/05 USCC hearing*. The Commission's website, which includes these and other past hearings, is at [http://www.uscc.gov].

[10] Hearing On Military Modernization and Cross-Strait Balance, Hearing Before the U.S.China Economic and Security Review Commission, February 6, 2004. Washington, U.S. Govt. Print. Off., 2004. (Hereafter cited as 2/6/04 USCC hearing.)

[11] Roger Cliff et al., *Entering the Dragon's Lair: Chinese Antiaccess Strategies and Their Implications for the United States*. Santa Monica, CA, RAND Corporation, 2007. 129 pp. (MG-524-AF, RAND Project Air Force.) Evan S. Medeiros et al., *A New Direction for China's Defense Industry*. Santa Monica, CA, RAND Corporation, 2005. 304 pp. (MG334, RAND Project Air Force.) (Hereafter cited as *2007 RAND report* and *2005 RAND report*.)

[12] Chinese Military Power, Report of an Independent Task Force Sponsored by the Council on Foreign Relations Maurice R. Greenberg Center for Geoeconomic Studies. Washington, 2003. (Harold Brown, Chair, Joseph W. Prueher, Vice Chair, Adam Segal, Project Director) (Hereafter cited as 2003 CFR task force report.)

[13] An additional source of reference information on China's navy, particularly with regard to its organization, leadership, political system, doctrine, and training is, U.S. Department of the Navy, Office of Naval Intelligence, *China's Navy 2007*, Washington, 2007. 130 pp.

[14] Unless otherwise indicated, shipbuilding program information in this section is taken from *Jane's Fighting Ships 2006-2007*. Other sources of information on these shipbuilding programs may disagree regarding projected ship commissioning dates or other details, but sources present similar overall pictures regarding PLA Navy shipbuilding.

[15] Depending on their ranges, TBMs can be divided into short-, medium-, and intermediate-range ballistic missiles (SRBMs, MRBMs, and IRBMs, respectively).

[16] *2007 DOD CMP*, pp. 3 and 42.

[17] Annual Threat Assessment of the Director of National Intelligence, January 11, 2007, John D. Negroponte, Director of National Intelligence, p. 10.

[18] *2007 DOD CMP*, pp. 16-17. DOD also states: "China continues to explore the use of ballistic and cruise missiles for anti-access missions, including counter-carrier and land attack, and is working on reconnaissance and communication systems to improve command, control, and targeting." (*2007 DOD CMP*, p. 3.)

[19] Yihong Chang and Andrew Koch, "Is China Building A Carrier?" *Jane's Defence Weekly*, August 17, 2005.

[20] 2007 DOD CMP, p. 17.

[21] Current and Projected National Security Threats to the United States, Vice Admiral Lowell E. Jacoby, U.S. Navy, Director, Defense Intelligence Agency, Statement for the Record [before the] Senate Select Committee on Intelligence, 16 February 2005, p. 13. See also Current and Projected National Security Threats to the United States, Vice Admiral Lowell E. Jacoby, U.S. Navy, Director, Defense Intelligence Agency, Statement For the Record [before the] Senate Armed Services Committee, 17 March 2005, p. 13.

[22] *2007 DOD CMP*, p. 17. For a recent article discussing China's ASCMs, see Robert Hewson, "Dragon's Teeth — Chinese Missiles Raise Their Game," *Jane's Navy International*, January/February 2007: 19-23.

[23] See, for example, Figure 7 (the map entitled "Taiwan Strait SAM coverage") in *2007 DOD CMP*, p. 31.

[24] UCAV means unmanned combat aerial vehicle (i.e., an armed UAV).

[25] *2007 DOD CMP*, p. 18. The report states further that "The Israelis transferred HARPY UCAVs to China in 2001 and conducted maintenance on HARPY parts during 2003-2004. In 2005, Israel began to improve government oversight of exports to China by strengthening controls of military exports, establishing controls on dual-use exports, and increasing the role of the Ministry of Foreign Affairs in export-related decisions." (Page 28)

[26] For a detailed discussion of China's submarine modernization program and a strong expression of concern regarding the implications of this effort for Taiwan and the United States, see the statement of Lyle J. Goldstein and William Murray as printed in *2/6/04 USCC hearing*, pp. 129-156. Goldstein and Murray's written statement was also published as a journal article; see Lyle Goldstein and William Murray, "Undersea Dragons, China's Maturing Submarine Force," *International Security*, Spring 2004, pp. 161-196. See also Richard R. Burgess, "Sub Reliance," *Seapower*, February 2007: 20-22.

[27] A previous CRS report discussed these four Kilo-class boats at length. See CRS Report RL30700, *China's Foreign Conventional Arms Acquisitions: Background and Analysis*, by Shirley Kan (Coordinator), Christopher Bolkcom, and Ronald O'Rourke.

[28] Some sources project that the final Kilos would be delivered in 2007 rather than 2006.

[29] There are also reports that the Kilos might also be armed with the Shkval, a Russian-made, supercavitating, high-speed torpedo, and that China might be building its own supercavitating torpedoes. (Statement of Lyle J. Goldstein and William Murray as printed in *2/6/04 USCC hearing*, p. 139.) A supercavitating torpedo surrounds itself with an envelope of gas bubbles, which dramatically reduces its resistance as it moves through the water, thereby permitting very high underwater speeds. The Shkval has a reported speed of 200 knots or more.

[30] One observer states that older and less sophisticated submarines will likely be employed to screen the higher-value assets. Chinese sources openly describe using certain submarines as "bait." Employing this tactic, it is conceivable that United States submarines could reveal their own presence to lurking Kilos by executing attacks against nuisance Mings and Romeos. No wonder China continues to operate the vessels, which are widely derided as obsolete by Western observers. The threat from these older submarines cannot be dismissed out of hand. Informal United States Navy testimony suggests that the PLAN can operate the older classes of diesel submarines with surprising tactical efficiency. (Statement of Lyle J. Goldstein and William Murray as printed in *2/6/04 USCC hearing*, p. 153)

[31] *2004 ONI WMC*, p. 11. The range of 25 to 50 is based on visual inspection of the graph.

[32] Andrew S. Erickson and Lyle J. Goldstein, "China's Future Submarine Force: Insights From Chinese Writings," *Naval War College Review*, Winter 2007: 55.

[33] John J. Tkacik, Jr., *China's Quest for a Superpower Military*, Heritage Foundation Backgrounder No. 2036, May 17, 2007, pp. 9-10. A footnote at the end of this quoted passage states: "Including at least five Type-94 Jins, five Type-093 Shangs, five Type-095s, one Yuan, 13 Songs, and 13 Kilo 877s and 636s."

[34] Federation of American Scientists (FAS), "China's Submarine Fleet Continues Low Patrol Rate," published online at [http://fas.org/blog/ssp/2007/02/].

[35] Federation of American Scientists (FAS), "China's Submarine Fleet Continues Low Patrol Rate," published online at [http://fas.org/blog/ssp/2007/02/].

[36] John J. Tkacik, Jr., *China's Quest for a Superpower Military*, Heritage Foundation Backgrounder No. 2036, May 17, 2007, pp. 9 and 10.

[37] *2007 DOD CMP*, pp. 22-24. Brackets and ellipses as in the original

[38] Andrew S. Erickson and Andrew R. Wilson, "China's Aircraft Carrier Dilemma," *Naval War College Review*, Autumn 2006: 13-45.

[39] A previous CRS report discussed the PLA Navy's first two Sovremenny-class destroyers and their SS-N-22 ASCMs at length. See CRS Report RL30700, op. cit.

[40] *2007 DOD CMP*, p. 3. The DOD report spells Sovremenny with two "y"s at the end.

[41] AAW is a term most frequently found in discussions of naval systems. Discussions of systems in other military services tend to use the term air defense.

[42] One observer states: It is of note that the Chinese navy has chosen to adopt an incremental approach, in which only two ships of each class are built, rather than opt for a longer shipbuilding line with corresponding economies in development and building costs and equipment commonality. A possible explanation is that the navy is on a steep learning curve and that, rather than being cautious about the introduction of new technology, it is keen to ensure that every ship introduced into service reflects the latest developments. (*Jane's Fighting Ships 2006-2007*, p. 30 (Executive Overview)) Another set of observers states that "China was forced to cancel its production of the Luhu class of destroyers because the U.S.-made gas turbine engines were no longer available after the United States imposed export restrictions on military-related goods following the Tiananmen Square incident in 1989. China's newest operational destroyers use Ukrainian, not Chinese, engines." (*2005 RAND report*, p. 140.)

[43] 2007 DOD CMP, pp. 3-4

[44] For a detailed article about the Luyang II class, see James C. Bussert, "China Debuts Aegis Destroyers," *Signal*, July 2005, pp. 59-62. See also *Fisher 7/27/05 testimony*, p. 12.

[45] 2007 DOD CMP, p. 3.

[46] *Jane's Fighting Ships 2006-2007*, also states: "Production of Jiangkai (Type 054) frigates has paused, possibly due to technical problems, although building of more advanced variants is expected." (Page 30 (Executive Overview).)

[47] France sold a modified version of the La Fayette-class design to Taiwan; the six ships that Taiwan built to the design entered service in 1996-1998. See also *Fisher 7/27/05 testimony*, pp. 12-13. One observer views the Jiangwei II-class ships as roughly comparable to France's Georges Leygues-class destroyer design, which entered service in 1979, Italy's Maestrale-class frigate design, which entered service in 1982, and the UK's Type 21 frigates, which entered service in starting in 1975 and were transferred to Pakistan in 19931994. (Massimo Annati, "China's PLA Navy, The Revolution," *Naval Forces*, No. 6, 2004, pp. 66-67.)

[48] *Jane's Fighting Ships 2006-2007*, p. 30 (Executive Overview). See also *Fisher 7/27/05 testimony*, p. 13; "PRC Appears Ready To Field New Trimaran Fast Missile Warship," *Defense and Foreign Affairs Daily*, October 5, 2004; Yihong Chang, "First Sight Of Chinese Catamaran," *Jane's Defense Weekly*, May 26, 2004.

[49] Jane's Fighting Ships 2006-2007, p. 30 (Executive Overview)

[50] 2004 ONI WMC, p. 19.

[51] 2003 DOD CMP, p. 27.

[52] *2002 DOD CMP*, p. 23. In 2000, DOD stated: The PLAN's mine stockpiles include vintage Russian moored-contact and bottom influence mines, as well as an assortment of domestically built mines. China currently produces the EM11 bottom-influence mine; the EM31 moored mine; the EM32 moored influence mine; the EM52 rocket-propelled rising mine; and, the EM-53 ship-laid bottom influence mine which is remotely controlled by a shore station. China is believed to have available acoustically activated remote control technology for its EM53. This technology probably could be used with other Chinese ship-laid mines including the EM52. Application of this technology could allow entire mines to be laid in advance of hostilities in a dormant position and activated or deactivated when required. China reportedly has completed development of a mobile mine and may be producing improved variants of Russian bottom mines and moored-influence mines. Over the next decade, China likely will attempt to acquire advanced propelled-warhead mines, as well as submarine-launched mobile bottom mines. (Department of Defense, *Annual Report On The Military Power of the People's*

Republic Of China, 2000. Washington, 2000. See the subsection on subsurface warfare.)

[53] Statement of Lyle J. Goldstein and William Murray as printed in *2/6/04 USCC hearing*, p. 133. See also p. 152.

[54] See *2005 DOD CMP*, p. 36; *2003 CFR task force report*, pp. 55-56; Peter Brookes, "The Art Of (Cyber) War, *New York Post*, August 29, 2005; Bradley Graham, "Hackers Attack Via Chinese websites," *Washington Post*, August 25, 2005: 1; Frank Tiboni, "The New Trojan War," *Federal Computer Week*, August 22, 2005: 60.

[55] Eric McVadon, as quoted in Dave Ahearn, "U.S. Can't Use Trade Imbalance To Avert China Invasion Of Taiwan," *Defense Today*, August 2, 2005, pp. 1-2.

[56] *2007 DOD CMP*, pp. 21-22.

[57] Current and Projected National Security Threats to the United States, Lieutenant General Michael D. Maples, U.S. Army, Director, Defense Intelligence Agency, Statement for the Record, Senate Select Committee on Intelligence Committee [sic], 11 January 2007, p. 28.

[58] For a general discussion of the potential role of nuclear weapons in notional crisis and conflict situations involving China, see CRS Report RL33607, *U.S. Conventional Forces and Nuclear Deterrence: A China Case Study*, by Christopher Bolkcom, Shirley A. Kan, and Amy F. Woolf.

[59] Following the April 1, 2001, collision in international airspace off China's coast of a U.S. Navy EP-3 electronic surveillance aircraft and a PLA F-8 fighter, which many observers believed was caused by reckless flying by the pilot of the F-8, China attempted to convince others that the collision was caused by poor flying by the pilot of the slower-flying and less maneuverable U.S. EP-3. For more on this event, see CRS Report RL30946, *China-U.S. Aircraft Collision Incident of April 2001: Assessments and Policy Implications*, by Shirley A. Kan, coordinator.

[60] See CRS Report RL32544, High Altitude Electromagnetic Pulse (HEMP) and High Power Microwave (HPM) Devices: Threat Assessments, by Clay Wilson; (Hereafter cited as CRS Report RL32544.) and John S. Foster, Jr., et al., Report of the Commission to Assess the Threat to the United States from Electromagnetic Pulse (EMP) Attack, Volume 1: Executive Report 2004. Washington, 2004, 53 pp. (Hereafter cited as 2004 EMP commission report.) See also the transcripts and written statements of hearings on EMP held before the House Armed Services Committee on July 22, 2004, and before the Military Research and Development Subcommittee of the House Armed Services Committee on October 7,

1999, and July 16, 1997. (In 1997, the full committee was called the House National Security Committee.)

[61] For more on HPM weapons, see CRS Report RL32544.

[62] One source states that "a 2,000-pound microwave munition will have a minimum radius [of effect] of approximately 200 meters," or roughly 650 feet. ("High-power microwave (HPM)/E-Bomb," available on the Internet at [http://www.globalsecurity.org/military/ systems/munitions/hpm.htm].) A second source says HPM weapons might have effective radii "on the order of hundreds of meters, subject to weapon performance and target set electrical hardness." (Section 4.1 of Carlo Kopp, "The Electromagnetic Bomb — a Weapon of Electrical Mass Destruction," available on the Internet at [http://www.globalsecurity.org/military/library/report/ 1996/apjemp.htm]. A third source states that "a small RF device might have a range measured in feet, while a relatively large RF device might produce upset or damage in electronics systems at a range measured in hundreds of feet, and interference at a range of hundreds of miles." (Statement of William R. Graham, Ph.D., before the Military Research and Development Subcommittee of the House Armed Services Committee, October 7, 1999.)

[63] One source states that: An electromagnetic warhead detonated within lethal radius of a surface combatant will render its air defence system inoperable, as well as damaging other electronic equipment such as electronic countermeasures, electronic support measures and communications. This leaves the vessel undefended until these systems can be restored, which may or may not be possible on the high seas. Therefore launching an electromagnetic glidebomb on to a surface combatant, and then reducing it with laser or television guided weapons is an alternate strategy for dealing with such targets. (Section 10.4 of Carlo Kopp, "The Electromagnetic Bomb — a Weapon of Electrical Mass Destruction," op. cit.) For additional discussion HPM weapons at sea, see Massimo Annati, "Non-Lethal Weapons: Their Application in the Maritime World," *Naval Forces*, No. 1, 2006, particularly pages 50, 51, and 53.

[64] See the sections entitled "Reducing the PLA by 200,000," "Implementing the Strategic Project for Talented People," "Intensifying Joint Training," and "Deepening Logistical Reforms," in Chapter II on national defense policy.

[65] 2005 DOD CMP, p. 26.

[66] 2007 DOD CMP, p. 5.

References

[67] See, for example, *2005 DOD CMP*, pp. 5-6; the statement of David M. Finkelstein as printed in *2/6/04 USCC hearing*, p. 90-93; and *2003 CFR task force report*, pp. 38-39.

[68] See, for example, [Statement of] Dennis J. Blasko, Independent Consultant, September 15, 2005, Hearing on "Net Assessment of Cross-Strait Military Capabilities" Before the U.S.-China Economic and Security Review Commission; the statement by Lyle J. Goldstein and William Murray as printed in *2/6/04 USCC hearing*, pp. 131-132, 143-145; and *2003 CFR task force report*, pp. 39-41, 45-46, 49.

[69] Regarding reformed logistics, see *2005 DOD CMP*, p. 34, and the statement of Lyle J. Goldstein and William Murray as printed in *2/6/04 USCC hearing*, p. 145.

[70] Council on Foreign Relations, *U.S.-China Relations: An Affirmative Agenda, A responsible Course*, Report of an Independent Task Force sponsored by the Council on Foreign Relations, Washington, 2007, p. 47.

[71] Current and Projected National Security Threats to the United States, Vice Admiral Lowell E. Jacoby, U.S. Navy, Director, Defense Intelligence Agency, Statement for the Record [before the] Senate Select Committee on Intelligence, 16 February 2005, p. 16. See also Current and Projected National Security Threats to the United States, Vice Admiral Lowell E. Jacoby, U.S. Navy, Director, Defense Intelligence Agency, Statement For the Record [before the] Senate Armed Services Committee, 17 March 2005, p. 16.

[72] 2003 CFR task force report, pp. 28 and 47.

[73] *2005 RAND report*, pp. 110-111. On page 153, the report similarly states that China's SBI [shipbuilding industry] exhibits a number of limitations and weaknesses that will constrain naval modernization. Although the design and construction of vessels have improved, the SBI has experienced numerous problems producing quality subsystems for both merchant and naval vessels. Chinese shipbuilders have had to rely heavily on foreign imports for the power plants, navigation and sensor suites, and key weapon systems for its newest naval platforms. For example, Chinese marine-engine factories have had difficulties producing gas turbine engines powerful enough for large destroyers and related combatants. The last two classes of Chinese destroyers have relied on imported gas turbine engines, for example. This high degree of reliance on foreign goods creates major challenges for systems integration and, given the inconsistent availability of certain weapon systems, complicates serial production of some platforms.

[74] *2005 RAND report*, p. 139-140. On pages 153-154, the report similarly states that Chinese combatants lack long-range air-defense systems, modern anti — submarine warfare (ASW) weapons, and advanced electronic warfare capabilities needed to outfit its new ships. China's other defense sectors have been slow to produce modern versions of these crucial technologies beyond copies or modifications of Soviet or Western systems. For example, Chinese firms have experienced several delays in the indigenous production of a medium and long-range SAM system for naval area defense, which has complicated the completion of some naval projects.... [T]his situation is changing as China's defense-industrial complex modernizes. But, some past weaknesses persist and, over the medium term, they will continue to constrain China's ability to project and sustain naval power for extended periods in the coming decade.

[75] This is a reference to an April 2003 fatal accident aboard a Ming-class boat with hull number 361. See Appendix A for additional details concerning this accident.

[76] Statement of Lyle J. Goldstein and William Murray as printed in *2/6/04 USCC hearing*, p. 156.

[77] *2007 DOD CMP*, p. 1 (Executive Summary).

[78] *2005 DOD CMP*, executive summary and pp. 33-34.

[79] *2007 DOD CMP*, p. 15.

[80] [Statement of] Rear Admiral (U.S. Navy, Retired) Eric A. McVadon, Director of Asia-Pacific Studies, Institute for Foreign Policy Analysis, Consultant on East Asia Security Affairs, Before the U.S.-China Economic and Security Review Commission, [regarding] Recent Trends in China's Military Modernization, 15 September 2005, p. 6. (Hereafter cited as *McVadon 9/15/05 testimony*.) Italics as in the original.

[81] The passage at this point is quoting from the 2003 edition of DOD's annual report on China's military power (*2003 DOD CMP*, p. 25).

[82] Dominic DeSciscciolo, "Red Aegis," *U.S. Naval Institute Proceedings*, July 2004, pp. 5658.

[83] Massimo Annati, "China's PLA Navy, The Revolution," *Naval Forces*, No. 6, 2004, p. 75.

[84] Ibid., p. 73.

[85] *2005 DOD CMP*, pp. 34-35.

[86] James C. Bussert, "China Builds Destroyers Around Imported Technology," *Signal*, August 2004, p. 67.

[87] The white paper states: The PLA will promote coordinated development of firepower, mobility and information capability, enhance the development of its operational strength with priority given to the Navy, Air Force and Second Artillery Force, and strengthen its comprehensive deterrence and warfighting capabilities.... The Army is streamlined by reducing the ordinary troops that are technologically backward while the Navy, Air Force and Second Artillery Force are strengthened.... While continuing to attach importance to the building of the Army, the PLA gives priority to the building of the Navy, Air Force and Second Artillery Force to seek balanced development of the combat force structure, in order to strengthen the capabilities for winning both command of the sea and command of the air, and conducting strategic counter-strikes. (*2004 China White Paper*, op cit, Chapter II national defense policy.)

[88] *2006 China White Paper*, paragraph entitled "Downsizing the PLA."

[89] *2006 China White Paper*, paragraphs entitled "Implementing the military strategy of active defense," and "Improving the structure of services and arms," and a paragraph in he section entitled "Development of the Services and Arms."

[90] See, for example, *2005 DOD CMP*, p. 1.

[91] U.S. Department of the Navy, Office of Naval Intelligence, *China's Navy 2007*, Washington, 2007. p. 11.

[92] Analysts disagree regarding China's potential for mounting an effective blockade, particularly with its submarine force. For an analysis that casts a skeptical eye on the potential, see Michael A. Glosny, "Strangulation from the Sea? A PRC Submarine Blockade of Taiwan," *International Security*, spring 2004, pp. 125-160. For an analysis that expresses more concern about this potential, see the statement of Lyle J. Goldstein and William Murray as printed in *2/6/04 USCC hearing*, pp. 132-133, 147-151. See also Michael C. Grubb, "Merchant Shipping In A Chinese Blockade Of Taiwan," Naval War College Review, *Winter 2007*: 81-102.

[93] *2007 DOD CMP*, pp. 32-33. DOD further notes that Amphibious operations are logistics-intensive, and their success depends upon air and sea superiority in the vicinity of the operation, the rapid buildup of supplies and sustainment on shore, and an uninterrupted fl ow of support thereafter. An amphibious campaign of the scale outlined in the Joint Island Landing Campaign would tax the capabilities of China's armed forces and almost certainly invite international intervention. Add to these strains the combat attrition of China's forces, and the complex tasks of urban warfare and counterinsurgency — assuming a successful landing

and breakout — and an amphibious invasion of Taiwan would be a significant political and military risk for China's leaders." (Pages 32-33) See also *2003 CFR task force report*, pp. 2, 3, and 53.

[94] See, for example, Eric A. McVadon, "Alarm Bells Ring as China Builds up its Armoury on a Massive Sale," *Jane's Defence Weekly*, March 16, 2005, p. 23; Edward Cody, "China Builds A Smaller, Stronger Military," *Washington Post*, April 12, 2005, p. 1; Bryan Bender, "China Bolsters Its Forces, US Says," *Boston Globe*, April 10, 2005, p. 1; Jim Yardley and Thom Shanker, "Chinese Navy Buildup Gives Pentagon New Worries," *New York Times*, April 8, 2005.

[95] 2007 DOD CMP, p. 32.

[96] *2007 DOD CMP*, pp. 15-18. Another observer states that This mission, in essence, is to be able quickly to overwhelm Taiwan's military, cow the Taiwan government, and deter, delay, or complicate effective and timely U.S. intervention.... The concept is ... to be able very rapidly, in a matter of days, to cause Taiwan to capitulate, with such capitulation abetted by the failure of the U.S. to respond promptly and effectively. As has been said often, Beijing's concept is to be able to present to Washington and the world a *fait accompli* concerning Taiwan.... Beijing has ... developed a concept to use force, if it feels it must, to defeat Taiwan, deter or delay U.S. intervention, and at least cause Japan to think twice before introducing overt military assistance in a developing crisis.... There is, in my opinion, no question that this is Beijing's concept for overwhelming Taiwan and deterring or confronting U.S. forces. (*McVadon 9/15/05 testimony*, pp. 1, 2, 2-3, 6.) See also Statement of Cortez A. Cooper III for *3/16/06 USCC hearing*, p. 3.

[97] Testimony of Fu S. Mei, Director, Taiwan Security Analysis Center (TAISAC), Before the U.S.-China Economic and Security Review Commission [regarding] "Taiwan Straits Issues and Chinese Military-Defense Budget," September 15, 2005, p. 3.

[98] One observer states: By 2008, China will have the capability to credibly conduct short-term sea denial operations out to about 400 nautical miles from its coastline; and by 2010 may be able to sustain such operations for a few weeks. Obviously, this capability does not accrue to the Straits of Malacca and the Indian Ocean — China can at best hope to "show the flag" for coercive and/or defensive purposes in those waters until after 2015. (Statement of Cortez A. Cooper III for *3/16/06 USCC hearing*, p.3.) This observer also states: Looking at a net assessment of emerging Chinese capabilities and U.S. power projection in the Pacific theater, there

is a window of concern between roughly 2008 and 2015. Many Chinese programs focused on Taiwan and the near periphery (new cruise and maneuverable ballistic missiles, submarines, and destroyers) will be fully online around 2008; but some of the US capabilities to defeat China's sea denial strategy (missile defenses, littoral strike assets, a state-of-the-art, integrated ASW network) may not be in place until around the middle of the next decade. (Ibid., p. 8.) Another observer states: Because the Chinese submarine fleet will operate in nearby waters and in the mid-Pacific, China need not wait until 2020 to challenge the U.S. at sea. It will likely have a home-field advantage in any East Asian conflict contingency as early as 2010, while the U.S. fleet will still have operational demands in the Middle East, and in tracking Russian ballistic missile submarines elsewhere. (*Tkacik 7/27/05 testimony*, p. 8.) See also *Fisher 7/27/05 testimony*, which cites the year 2010 on pages 3, 4, 7, 9 (twice), 11, and 16 in discussing China's military modernization and the resulting impact on the regional military balance, and Fisher's statement as printed in *2/6/04 USCC hearing*, p. 85, which states, "It is possible that before the end of the decade the PLA will have the capability to coordinate mass missile attacks on U.S. Naval Forces by submarines and Su-30s," and p. 88, which prints his table summarizing potential PLA anti-carrier forces by 2010.

[99] *2007 DOD CMP*, p. 15. Another observer states: "QDR [Quadrennial Defense Review] planners have recently moved forward (to 2012) their estimate of when key warfighting capabilities might be needed to fight China, and have postulated conflict scenarios lasting as long as seven years." (Loren B. Thompson, "Pentagon Fighter Study Raises Questions," August 22, 2005. Lexington Institute Issue Brief.) *2003 CFR task force report* discusses the difficulty of assessing the pace at which China's military modernization is occurring and presents a series of indicators on pages 11-15 (and again on pages 64-68) that can be monitored to help gauge the pace and direction of China's military modernization.

[100] For more on this topic, see CRS Report RL31183, *China's Maritime Territorial Claims: Implications for U.S. Interests*, Kerry Dumbaugh, coordinator. See also Chris Johnson, "Analysts Discuss Maritime Implications of China's Energy Strategy," *Inside the Navy*, December 18, 2006.

[101] See, for example, Statement of Cortez A. Cooper III for *3/16/06 USCC hearing*, p. 3; *Fisher 7/27/05 testimony*, p. 4; *McVadon 9/15/05 testimony*, p. 1; *2003 CFR task force report*, pp. 24-25, 31-32, 62-63; Edward Cody, "China Builds A Smaller, Stronger Military," April 12, 2005, p. 1; David Lague, "China's Growing Undersea Fleet Presents Challenge To Its Neighbors," *Wall Street Journal*, November 29, 2004. See also Chris Johnson, "Analysts Discuss Maritime Implications of China's Energy Strategy," *Inside the Navy*, December 18, 2006.

[102] *2007 DOD CMP*, p. I (Executive Summary).

[103] *2007 DOD CMP*, p. 15.

[104] *2007 DOD CMP*, pp. 8-9.

[105] *2007 DOD CMP*, pp. 22-24.

[106] Annual Threat Assessment of the Director of National Intelligence, January 11, 2007, John D. Negroponte, Director of National Intelligence, p. 10.

[107] Council on Foreign Relations, *U.S.-China Relations: An Affirmative Agenda, A responsible Course*, Report of an Independent Task Force sponsored by the Council on Foreign Relations, Washington, 2007, p. 43.

[108] Eric A. McVadon, "U.S.-PRC Maritime Cooperation: An Idea Whose Time Has Come," *China Brief (Jamestown Foundation)*, June 13, 2007.

[109] Mark Magnier, "China Regrets Sub Incident, Japan Says," *Los Angeles Times*, November 17, 2004; Martin Fackler, "Japanese Pursuit Of Chinese Sub Raises Tensions," *Wall Street Journal*, November 15, 2004: 20; Kenji Hall, "Japan: Unidentified sub is Chinese," *NavyTimes.com (Associated Press)*, November 12, 2004. See also *2006 DOD CMP*, pp. 1112.

[110] Current and Projected National Security Threats to the United States, Vice Admiral Lowell E. Jacoby, U.S. Navy, Director, Defense Intelligence Agency, Statement for the Record [before the] Senate Select Committee on Intelligence, 16 February 2005, p. 16-17. See also Current and Projected National Security Threats to the United States, Vice Admiral Lowell E. Jacoby, U.S. Navy, Director, Defense Intelligence Agency, Statement For the Record [before the] Senate Armed Services Committee, 17 March 2005, p. 17.

[111] Timothy Hu, "Ready, steady, go...," *Jane's Defence Weekly*, April 13, 2005: 27; "China Sub Tracked By U.S. Off Guam Before Japan Intrusion," *Japan Times*, November 17, 2004.

References

[112] Norimitsu Onishi and Howard W. French, "Japan's Rivalry With China Is Stirring A Crowded Sea," *New York Times*, September 11, 2005. See also "Japan Upset Over Chinese Warships Near Disputed Area," *DefenseNews.com*, October 3, 2005.

[113] "China Sends Warships to East China Sea," *DefenseNews.com*, September 29, 2005. *2006 DOD CMP*, p. 2, states that in the Fall of 2005, "PLA Navy vessels trained their weapons on Japanese Self Defense Forces aircraft monitoring Chinese drilling and survey activity in the disputed area."

[114] Bill Gertz, "China Sub Secretly Stalked U.S. Fleet," *Washington Times*, November 13, 2006: 13; Philip Creed, "Navy Confirms Chinese Sub Spotted Near Carrier," *NavyTimes.com*, November 13, 2006; Bill Gertz, "Defenses On [sic] Subs To Be Reviewed," *Washington Times*, November 14, 2006; En-Lai Yeoh, "Fallon Confirms Chinese Stalked Carrier," *NavyTimes.com*, November 14, 2006; Bill Gertz, "Admiral Says Sub Risked A Shootout," *Washington Times*, November 15, 2006; Jeff Schogol, "Admiral Disputes Report That Kitty Hawk, Chinese Sub Could Have Clashed," *Mideast Starts and Stripes*, November 17, 2006.

[115] Associated Press, "China Denies Reports That Sub Followed Kitty Hawk," *NavyTimes.com*, November 16, 2006. A shorter version of the same story was published as Associated Press, "China Denies Sub Followed A Group Of U.S. Warships," *Asian Wall Street Journal*, November 17, 2006: 11.

[116] Bill Gertz, "Defenses On [sic] Subs To Be Reviewed," *Washington Times*, November 14, 2006: 1. One observer recounts the incident as follows: In September 2006, Rear Admiral Ding Yiping, China's top submarine officer and PLAN Vice Chief of Staff, sent a Song submarine on a mission to hunt an American carrier. On October 27 (October 26, Washington time), the submarine surfaced in waters off Okinawa within torpedo range of the U.S.S. Kitty Hawk, where it was seen in the Kitty Hawk's wake by an F-18 pilot on landing approach. It then submerged and disappeared, defeating all U.S. anti-submarine warfare (ASW) efforts to detect it. The carrier battle group's ASW systems did not detect the sub because it had apparently waited — submerged, stationary, and silent — for at least oneday as the task force approached the area. Beijing's state-controlled media reported that Admiral Ding had personally commanded the entire operation, perhaps even skippering the submarine himself, and predicted that the success of his mission would lead to a promotion.... The official Chinese press noted the PLA high command's confidence in Admiral

Ding — ample evidence of their pleasure at the success the mission against the Kitty Hawk. The Chinese foreign ministry's protest that the vessel had not stalked the Kitty Hawk is likely the literal truth, indicating that the submarine simply waited submerged until the U.S. battle group sailed over it. (John J. Tkacik, Jr., *China's Quest for a Superpower Military*, Heritage Foundation Backgrounder No. 2036, May 17, 2007, pp. 9 and 10.)

[117] Bill Gertz, "China Builds Up Strategic Sea Lanes," *Washington Times*, January 18, 2005, p.1. The report stated that China is: According to the article, The Pentagon report said China, by militarily controlling oil shipping sea lanes, could threaten ships, "thereby creating a climate of uncertainty about the safety of all ships on the high seas." The report noted that the vast amount of oil shipments through the sea lanes, along with growing piracy and maritime terrorism, prompted China, as well as India, to build up naval power at "chokepoints" along the sea routes from the Persian Gulf to the South China Sea. "China ... is looking not only to build a blue-water navy to control the sea lanes, but also to develop undersea mines and missile capabilities to deter the potential disruption of its energy supplies from potential threats, including the U.S. Navy, especially in the case of a conflict with Taiwan," the report said.... "The Iraq war, in particular, revived concerns over the impact of a disturbance in Middle Eastern supplies or a U.S. naval blockade," the report said, noting that Chinese military leaders want an ocean-going navy and "undersea retaliatory capability to protect the sea lanes." China believes the U.S. military will disrupt China's energy imports in any conflict over Taiwan, and sees the United States as an unpredictable country that violates others' sovereignty and wants to "encircle" China, the report said. See also Edward Cody, "China Builds A Smaller, Stronger Military," *Washington Post*, April 12, 2005, p. 1.

[118] For discussions relating to Taiwan's potential military capabilities in such a scenario, see CRS Report RL30957, *Taiwan: Major U.S. Arms Sales Since 1990*; and CRS Report RL30341, *China/Taiwan: Evolution of the 'One China' Policy — Key Statements from Washington, Beijing, and Taipei*, both by Shirley A. Kan.

[119] For a discussion, see archived CRS Report 92-803, *Naval Forward Deployments and the Size of the Navy*, by Ronald O'Rourke. See Table 1. (Out of print and available directly from the author.)

[120] The other ships include amphibious ships and mine countermeasures ships.

References

[121] One of these SSNs, the San Francisco, was significantly damaged in a collision with an undersea mountain near Guam in January 2005. The ship was transferred to the Puget Sound Naval Shipyard at Bremerton, WA, for repairs, and is to be replaced at Guam by another SSN, the Buffalo, in July 2007.

[122] For a discussion see CRS Report RS21338, *Navy Ship Deployments: New Approaches* — Background and Issues for Congress, by Ronald O'Rourke.

[123] Other potential Western Pacific locations, at least in theory, include South Korea (where other U.S. forces have been based for years), the Philippines (where the U.S. Navy ships used as a major repair port until the early 1990s), and Australia.

[124] U.S. Navy ships visit Singapore, and there is a U.S. Navy logistic group there, but no U.S. Navy ships are currently homeported at Singapore.

[125] Everett is located on the Puget Sound, about 23 nautical miles north of Seattle.

[126] DOD decided to home port the carrier in question, the Carl Vinson, at San Diego.

[127] China's Military Modernization and the Cross-Strait Balance, [Statement of] Roger Cliff, September 2005, Testimony presented before the U.S.-China Economic and Security Review Commission on September 15, 2005, pp. 9-10. (Hereafter cited as *Cliff 9/15/05 testimony*.)

[128] For a list of recommended actions for improving the ability of bases in the Western Pacific to defend themselves from PLA attack, 2007 RAND report, pp. 95-101.

[129] See, for example, the statement of Lyle J. Goldstein and William Murray in *2/6/04 USCC hearing*, pp. 148, 150, and 152.

[130] Jason Ma, "ASW Concept Of Operations Sees 'Sensor Rich Way Of Fighting Subs," *Inside the Navy*, February 7, 2005. A January 2005 article stated: The Navy cannot fight diesel subs with "force on force," such as sending one sub to defeat another sub, because that is not cost effective, [Rear Admiral John Waickwicz, chief of Fleet Anti-Submarine Warfare Command] told *Inside the Navy*. For example, the new Virginia-class subs cost about $2 billion each, while advanced diesel subs cost hundreds of millions of dollars each. Instead of force on force, ASW tactics will emphasize using networked sensors and communications to allow one platform — like a sub, Littoral Combat Ship, or aircraft — to defeat multiple diesel subs, he said. "You have to be able to destroy them at a very large rate, because potential enemies may have a large number" of

subs, he explained. "We don't have that luxury to go one against one anymore," he added, noting that individual ASW platforms will rely on their greater capability to take on multiple subs. (Jason Ma, "Admiral: Navy's ASW Tactics To Be Aggressive And Offense-Minded," *Inside the Navy*, January 17, 2005.)

[131] Transcript of conference, as posted on the Internet by AEI at [http://www.aei.org/events/ filter.all,eventID.1051/transcript.asp]. An October 2004 article stated: more than just improving antisubmarine operations, Clark's goal is to "fundamentally change" ASW operations away from individual platforms — ship, submarine or aircraft — to a system with the attributes of "pervasive awareness, persistence and speed, all enabled by technological agility." To meet this goal, "we think we're going to have to go offboard of our platforms," using unmanned aerial, surface and underwater vehicles, and a network of distributed sensors to provide the identification and localization that would allow quick transition to the attack, [Rear Admiral Mark W. Kenny, the flag officer in charge of Task Force ASW] said. "That's what we're focused on: (finding) a high number of quiet contacts in a demanding environment with a timeline that requires us to gain access quickly." The task force has tested those concepts in at-sea experiments focused on distributive systems, which could be an array of easily deployed underwater sensors, passive and active, networked together and linked to manned platforms, he explained. Among them is the Advanced Deployable System, which the Program Executive Office for Integrated Warfare Systems currently is studying, along with such other ASW-related concepts as a multisensor Torpedo Recognition and Alertment Function Segment (previously known as Torpedo Recognition and Alertment Function Processor) and the Multifunction Towed Array to improve detection and tracking capability. (Otto Kreisher, "As Underwater Threat Re-Emerges, Navy Renews Emphasis On ASW," *Seapower*, October 2004, p. 15.)

[132] Jason Ma, "Autonomous ASW Sensor Field Seen As High-Risk Technical Hurdle," *Inside the Navy*, June 6, 2005. See also Jason Ma, "Navy's Surface Warfare Chief Cites Progress In ASW Development," *Inside the Navy*, January 17, 2005.

[133] See, for example, General Accounting Office, Navy Acquisitions[:] Improved Littoral War-Fighting Capabilities Needed, GAO-01-493, May 2001; and General Accounting Office, Navy Mine Warfare[:] Plans to Improve Countermeasures Capabilities Unclear, GAO/NSIAD-98-135, June 1998.

References

[134] The Navy's mine warfare plan is available on the Internet at [http://www.exwar.org/ Htm/4000.htm]. See also Department of the Navy, *Highlights of the Department of the Navy FY 2008 Budget*, Washington, 2007. (Office of Budget, February 2007) pp. 3-14.

[135] A November 2006 press report, quoting unnamed U.S. defense officials, stated that Admiral William Fallon, commander of the U.S. Pacific Command, "has restricted U.S. intelligence-gathering activities against China, fearing that disclosure of the activities would upset relations with Beijing. The restrictions are hindering efforts to know more about China's military buildup, the officials said." (Bill Gertz, "China Sub Secretly Stalked U.S. Fleet, *Washington Times*, November 13, 2006: 13.)

[136] Potential candidates include, among others, Spruance (DD-963) class destroyers, which could be reactivated as ASW platforms or missile shooters, Oliver Hazard Perry (FFG-7) class frigates and TAGOS-type ocean surveillance (i.e., towed-array sonar) ships, both of which could be reactivated as ASW platforms, and ASW-capable aircraft such as S-3 carrier-based airplanes and P-3 land-based maritime patrol aircraft.

[137] Additional measures that could assist in tracking PLA SSBNs include satellite surveillance (particularly when the SSBNs are in port or if they surface during their deployments) and human intelligence.

[138] For further discussion, see CRS Report RS22373, Navy Role in Global War on Terrorism (GWOT) — Background and Issues for Congress, by Ronald O'Rourke.

[139] Transcript of conference, as posted on the Internet by AEI at [http://www.aei.org/events/ filter.all,eventID.1051/transcript.asp].

[140] For a detailed discussion, see CRS Report RL32665, Navy Force Structure and Shipbuilding Plans: Background and Issues for Congress, by Ronald O'Rourke.

[141] U.S. Department of Defense, *Quadrennial Defense Review Report*. Washington, 2006. (February 6, 2006) p. 47.

[142] U.S. Congressional Budget Office, *Increasing the Mission Capability of the Attack Submarine Force*, Washington, CBO, 2002. (A CBO Study, March 2002), 41 pp.

[143] CRS Report RL32731, Navy Aircraft Carriers: Proposed Retirement of USS John F. Kennedy — Issues and Options for Congress, by Ronald O'Rourke.

[144] CRS Report RL32418, Navy Attack Submarine Force-Level Goal and Procurement Rate: Background and Issues for Congress, by Ronald O'Rourke.

[145] Andrew S. Erickson and Lyle J. Goldstein, "China's Future Submarine Force: Insights From Chinese Writings," *Naval War College Review*, Winter 2007: 55-56.

[146] Andrew S. Erickson and Lyle J. Goldstein, "China's Future Submarine Force: Insights From Chinese Writings," *Naval War College Review*, Winter 2007: 61.

[147] The quoted passage is referring at this point to the collision of the San Francisco with an undersea mountain near Guam — an accident that severely damaged the ship.

[148] Andrew S. Erickson and Lyle J. Goldstein, "China's Future Submarine Force: Insights From Chinese Writings," *Naval War College Review*, Winter 2007: 71. The first bracketed phrase identifying the San Francisco as a Los Angeles-class SSN was inserted by this CRS report for purposes of explanation; the second bracketed phrase referring to U.S. submarine production appears in the quoted passage.

[149] See, for example, John R. Benedict, "The Unraveling And Revitalization Of U.S. Navy Antisubmarine Warfare," *Naval War College Review*, spring 2005, pp. 93-120, particularly pp. 104-106; and the statement by Lyle J. Goldstein and William Murray in *2/6/04 USCC hearing*, pp. 149-150.

[150] See, for example, Jason Ma and Christopher J. Castelli, "Adaptation Of PAC-3 For Sea-Based Terminal Missile Defense Examined," *Inside the Navy*, July 19, 2004; Malina Brown, "Navy Rebuilding Case For Terminal Missile Defense Requirement," *Inside the Navy*, April 19, 2004.

[151] For more on the CG(X), see CRS Report RL32109, Navy DDG-1000 (DD(X)) and CG(X) Ship Acquisition Programs: Oversight Issues and Options for Congress, by Ronald O'Rourke.

[152] CRS Report RS22559, Navy CG(X) Cruiser Design Options: Background and Oversight Issues For Congress, by Ronald O'Rourke.

[153] Jefferson Morris, "Study Points To Need For More SM-3s, THAAD Interceptors," *Aerospace Daily and Defense Report*," May 17, 2007: 3.

[154] For more on the F-22, JSF, and F/A-18E/F, see CRS Report RL33543, Tactical Aircraft Modernization: Issues for Congress; CRS Report RL31673, F-22A Raptor; CRS Report RL30563, F-35 Joint Strike Fighter (JSF) Program: Background, Status, and Issues; and CRS Report RL30624, Military Aircraft, the F/A-18E/F Super Hornet Program: Background and Issues for Congress, all by Christopher Bolkcom.

References 117

[155] An article by an Air Force officer raises a related issue — whether Air Force aircraft have sufficient capability for attacking targets at sea to adequately assist Navy aircraft in countering Chinese naval forces operating in the Strait of Mallaca area as part of a "string of pearls" strategy. See Lawrence Spinetta, "Cutting China's 'Sting of Pearls,'" *U.S. Naval Institute Proceedings*, October 2006: 40-42.

[156] General Accounting Office, Navy Acquisitions[:] Improved Littoral War-Fighting Capabilities Needed, GAO-01-493, May 2001; and General Accounting Office, Defense Acquisitions[:] Comprehensive Strategy Needed to Improve Ship Cruise Missile Defense, GAO/NSIAD-00-149, July 2000.

[157] For more on CEC and NIFC-CA, see CRS Report RS20557, *Navy Network-Centric Warfare Concept: Key Programs and Issues for Congress*, by Ronald O'Rourke.

[158] The Navy is currently developing a new version of the Standard Missile called the SM-6 Extended Range Active Missile (ERAM) that will have a considerably longer range than the current SM-2 air defense missile. The SM-6 will also have an active seeker that will permit the missile to home in on the target on its own, without being illuminated by a ship-based radar, as is the case with the SM-2.

[159] An October 2005 report from the Defense Science Board (DSB) highlights "The dire need for several types of supersonic targets to represent existing anti-ship cruise missile threats." (Page 1) The report states: The Russians have produced and deployed a variety of supersonic, anti-ship cruise missiles. Some of these missiles are sea-skimming vehicles; others attack from high altitudes. At the time of the Task Force, the United States had zero capability to test its air defense systems such as AEGIS or Improved Sea Sparrow against supersonic targets, and the Task Force views this shortfall as the major deficiency in our overall aerial targets enterprise. Aggressive actions are needed to fix the problem. (Department of Defense, *Report of the Defense Science Board Task Force on Aerial Targets*. Washington, 2005. (October 2005, Office of the Under Secretary of Defense for Acquisition, Technology, and Logistics) pp. 2.) A cover memorandum attached to the report from William P. Delaney and General Michael Williams, USMC (Ret.), the co-chairmen of the task force, states: The area of greatest concern to the Task Force was our gap in supersonic anti-ship cruise missiles for testing. The Russians have deployed at least three such cruise missiles that involve either sea-skimming flight profiles or a high-altitude profile involving a power dive to the target. At this time,

we have no test vehicles for either flight profile. See also John Liang, "DSB Highlights 'Dire' Need For Supersonic Cruise Missile Targets," *Inside the Navy*, November 14, 2005.The lack of targets for fully emulating supersonic ASCMs has been an issue since the early 1980s, when the Navy first deployed the Aegis AAW system. See CRS Report 84-180, *The Aegis Anti-Air Warfare System: Its Principal Components, Its Installation On The CG-47 And DDG-51 Class Ships, And Its Effectiveness*, by Ronald O'Rourke. (October 24, 1984) pp. 16-17. (This report is out of print and is available directly from the author.)

[160] For more on the LCS, see CRS Report RL33741, Navy Littoral Combat Ship (LCS) Program: Oversight Issues and Options for Congress, by Ronald O'Rourke.

[161] Statement of Admiral Michael G. Mullen, Chief of Naval Operations, Before the House Armed Services Committee, 01 March 2007, pp. 8, 43-45.

[162] Christopher Munsey, "Fleet Anti-Sub Command Stands Up," *Navy Times*, April 19, 2004, p. 29. See also Audrey McAvoy, "U.S. Navy Puts New Emphasis On Anti-Submarine Training; New Threat From China Seen," *NavyTimes.com*, January 26, 2006; and a similar article by the same author, "USS Ronald Reagan Trains To Find Silent Threat," *Honolulu Star-Bulletin*, January 22, 2006.

[163] Jose Higuera, "Sweden's Gotland Heads For A Year With US Navy," *Jane's Navy International*, July/August 2005; 8; S. C. Irwin, "Swedish Submarine Expected To Enhance Navy's Antisubmarine Warfare Primacy," *Navy Newsstand*, June 20, 2005; Gidget Fuentes, "Swedish Sub To Drill With U.S. Navy For A Year," *DefenseNews.com*, May 18, 2005; "U.S., Swedish Navies Sign Agreement To Bilaterally Train On State-Of-The-Art Sub," *Navy Newsstand*, March 23, 2005.

[164] Christopher Munsey, "Colombian, Peruvian Subs To Take Part In Exercise," *NavyTimes.com*, April 14, 2005; Mark O. Piggott, "South American Submarines Enhance U.S. Navy's Fleet Readiness," *Navy Newsstand*, April 14, 2005.

[165] Jennifer H. Svan, "Pacific Fleet Commander: Sub Threats Top Priority," *Pacific Stars and Stripes*, October 3, 2005.

[166] Statement of Admiral Michael G. Mullen, Chief of Naval Operations, Before the House Armed Services Committee, 01 March 2007, p. 45.

[167] Current information on Navy mines and mine development programs is available on the Internet at [http://www.exwar.org/Htm/4000.htm].

References

[168] Harold Kennedy, "Navy Command Engages In Info Warfare Campaign," *National Defense*, November 2003. See also Frank Tiboni, "DOD's 'Manhattan Project'," *Federal Computer Week*, August 29, 2005.

[169] CRS Report RL32114, Computer Attack and Cyberterrorism: Vulnerabilities and Policy Issues for Congress, by Clay Wilson.

[170] *2004 EMP commission report*. The report of the commission stated on page 1 that "The high-altitude nuclear weapon-generated electromagnetic pulse (EMP) is one of a small number of threats that has the potential to hold our society seriously at risk and might result in defeat of our military forces." The report stated later that The end of the Cold War relaxed the discipline for achieving EMP survivability within the Department of Defense, and gave rise to the perception that an erosion of EMP survivability of military forces was an acceptable risk. EMP simulation and test facilities have been mothballed or dismantled, and research concerning EMP phenomena, hardening design, testing, and maintenance has been substantially decreased. However, the emerging threat environment, characterized by a wide spectrum of actors that include near-peers, established nuclear powers, rogue nations, sub-national groups, and terrorist organizations that either now have access to nuclear weapons and ballistic missiles or may have such access over the next 15 years have combined to place the risk of EMP attack and adverse consequences on the US to a level that is not acceptable. Current policy is to continue to provide EMP protection to strategic [i.e., long-range nuclear] forces and their controls; however, the end of the Cold War has relaxed the discipline for achieving and maintaining that capability within these forces.... The situation for general-purpose forces (GPF) is more complex.... Our increasing dependence on advanced electronics systems results in the potential for an increased EMP vulnerability of our technologically advanced forces, and if unaddressed makes EMP employment by an adversary an attractive asymmetric option. The United States must not permit an EMP attack to defeat its capability to prevail. The Commission believes it is not practical to protect all of the tactical forces of the US and its coalition partners from EMP in a regional conflict. A strategy of replacement and reinforcement will be necessary. However, there is a set of critical capabilities that is essential to tactical regional conflicts that must be available to these reinforcements. This set includes satellite navigation systems, satellite and airborne intelligence and targeting systems, an adequate communications infrastructure, and missile defense. The current capability to field a tactical force for regional conflict is

inadequate in light of this requirement. Even though it has been US policy to create EMP-hardened tactical systems, the strategy for achieving this has been to use the DoD acquisition process. This has provided many equipment components that meet criteria for durability in an EMP environment, but this does not result in confidence that fielded forces, as a system, can reliably withstand EMP attack. Adherence to the equipment acquisition policy also has been spotty, and the huge challenge of organizing and fielding an EMP-durable tactical force has been a disincentive to applying the rigor and discipline needed to do so. (Pages 47-48.)

[171] Source: Transcript of hearing.

[172] Ibid.

[173] Unless otherwise indicated, shipbuilding program information in this section is taken from *Jane's Fighting Ships 2006-2007*. Other sources of information on these shipbuilding programs may disagree regarding projected ship commissioning dates or other details, but sources present similar overall pictures regarding PLA Navy shipbuilding.

[174] *2004 ONI WMC*, p. 21. On Page 3 (Overview), ONI notes, without reference to any specific country, that "antiship ballistic missiles could be fired at our ships at sea."

[175] *2004 ONI WMC*, p. 22. Page 20 states: "Maneuvering reentry vehicles serve two purposes: one to provide an unpredictable target to complicate missile defense efforts and the other, potentially, to adjust missile flight path to achieve greater accuracy."

[176] Fisher 7/27/05 testimony, p. 6.

[177] Presentation entitled "Beijing Eye View of Strategic Landscale" by Mike McDevitt at a June 20, 2005, conference on the future of the U.S. Navy held in Washington, DC, by the American Enterprise Institute. Quote taken from McDevitt's notes for the presentation, which he provided to CRS.

[178] *McVadon 9/15/05 testimony*, pp. 4-5.

[179] *2004 ONI WMC*, pp. 25, 26.

[180] Testimony of Richard D. Fisher, Jr., for *3/16/06 USCC hearing*, p. 9.

[181] *2004 ONI WMC*, p. 23.

[182] *McVadon 9/15/05 testimony*, p. 5.

[183] *2007 DOD CMP*, p. 4

[184] Testimony of Richard D. Fisher, Jr., for *3/16/06 USCC* hearing, p. 11.

[185] *2007 DOD CMP*, p. 4.

[186] *2007 DOD CMP*, p. 18.

References

[187] *2004 ONI WMC*, p. 27. *Fisher 7/27/05 testimony*, pp. 3-4, 9-10.

[188] John J. Tkacik, Jr., *China's Quest for a Superpower Military*, Heritage Foundation Backgrounder No. 2036, May 17, 2007, pp. 13-14.

[189] *Fisher 7/27/05 testimony*, p. 11. On page 4, Fisher similarly states "It can be estimated that by 2010 the PLA Navy could have 50 to 60 nuclear and new conventional attack submarines...."

[190] McVadon 9/15/05 testimony, p. 5.

[191] Statement of Lyle J. Goldstein and William Murray as printed in *2/6/04 USCC hearing*, pp. 155-156.

[192] One news article, citing information from the Office of Naval Intelligence, states that a total of 5 are expected. (Bill Gertz, "China Expands Sub Fleet," *Washington Times*, March 2, 2007.)

[193] 2004 ONI WMC, p. 37.

[194] *2007 DOD CMP*, pp. 3, 19 (Figure 3), and 42 (Figure 14).

[195] 2007 DOD CMP, p. 19 (Figure 3). China also operates a single Xia (Type 092) class SSBN that entered service in 1987, and a single Golf (Type 031) non-nuclear-powered ballistic missile submarine (SSB) that entered service in the late 1960s. The Xia-class boat is armed with 12 CSS-N-3 (JL-1) SLBMs that have a range of roughly 1,200 nautical miles. The Golf-class boat is used as an SLBM test platform.

[196] Bill Gertz, "China Expands Sub Fleet," *Washington Times*, March 2, 2007.

[197] 2007 DOD CMP, p. 3.

[198] See, for example, Ronald O'Rourke, "Maintaining the Edge in US ASW," *Navy International*, July/August 1988, pp. 348-354.

[199] *2005 ONI WMC*, p. 14.

[200] Fisher 7/27/05 testimony, pp. 9, 11.

[201] Andrew S. Erickson and Lyle J. Goldstein, "China's Future Submarine Force: Insights From Chinese Writings," *Naval War College Review*, Winter 2007: 55-56.

[202] Andrew S. Erickson and Lyle J. Goldstein, "China's Future Submarine Force: Insights From Chinese Writings," *Naval War College Review*, Winter 2007: 67.

[203] Some sources project that the final Kilos would be delivered in 2007.

[204] 2004 ONI WMC, p. 12.

[205] Tkacik 7/27/05 testimony, p. 8. See also Fisher 7/27/05 testimony, pp. 11-12.

[206] *Jane's Fighting Ships 2005-2006*, for example, states: "It is fair to say that the intelligence community was caught completely unawares by the

emergence of the Yuan class...." *Jane's Fighting Ships 2005-2006*, p. 30 (Executive Overview). See also Bill Gertz, "Chinese Produce New Type Of Sub," *Washington Times*, July 16, 2004: 1.

[207] An AIP system, such as a fuel cell system or a closed-cycle diesel engine, extends the stationary or low-speed submerged endurance of a non-nuclear-powered submarine from a few days to perhaps two or three weeks. AIP technology does not extend the high-speed submerged endurance of a non-nuclear-powered submarine, which remains limited, due to battery capacity, to about 1 to 3 hours of high-speed operations.

[208] Fisher 7/27/05 testimony, p. 11.

[209] 2005 RAND report, pp. 148-149.

[210] "CHINA — Submarine Force Moving Forward," *Submarine Review*, April 2005: 106. rubber dampening tiles on the hull and shock absorbency for the engine to reduce its acoustic signature. The Song may also be able to launch cruise missiles when submerged, another design advance for China's conventional submarines. Seven Song-class vessels have reportedly been launched already, and additional ones have entered serial production at the Wuchang Shipyard in Wuhan. The rate of Song production has clearly increased in recent years.

[211] 2005 RAND report, p. 148.

[212] John J. Tkacik, Jr., China's Quest for a Superpower Military, Heritage Foundation Backgrounder No. 2036, May 17, 2007, pp. 12-13.

[213] Jane's Fighting Ships 2006-2007, p. 30 (Executive Overview)

[214] Testimony of Richard D. Fisher, Jr. For 3/16/06 USCC hearing, pp. 5-6. See also David Lague, "An Aircraft Carrier For China?" *International Herald-Tribune*, January 31, 2006; Norman Friedman, "Varyag Redux?" *U.S. Naval Institute Proceedings*, December 2005: 91.

[215] Yihong Chang and Andrew Koch, "Is China Building A Carrier?," *Jane's Defence Weekly*, August 17, 2005. See also Ian Storey and You Ji, "China's Aircraft Carrier Ambitions, Seeking Truth from Rumors," *Naval War College Review*, winter 2004, pp. 7793.

[216] VLCCs (very large crude carriers) and ULCCs (ultra-large crude carriers) are the two largest kinds of commercial crude oil tankers.

[217] *2005 RAND report*, pp. 149-150. See also Statement of Cortez A. Cooper III for *3/16/06 USCC hearing*, p. 5.

[218] Fisher 7/27/05 testimony, p. 12.

[219] *2005 RAND report*, p. 110. Similarly, the report states on page 140 that The expansion and modernization of China's shipbuilding industry contributed to the PLAN's efforts to design and build better naval

References

vessels.... These developments have enabled Chinese shipbuilders to build more-seaworthy and more reliable naval ships with better habitability, damage control facilities, engines, and electronics. In short, Chinese shipbuilders have become more efficient, better skilled, and more sophisticated in designing and building ships for the PLAN.

[220] 2005 RAND report, pp. 144-145.
[221] 2005 RAND report, pp. 146-147.
[222] Norman Friedman, "A New Role For Active Radar Arrays?" *U.S. Naval Institute Proceedings,* January 2006: 91.
[223] *2004 ONI WMC,* p. 29.
[224] *2005 RAND report,* p. 147.
[225] 2006 DOD CMP, p. 30. See also Fisher 7/27/05 testimony, p. 13.
[226] This is a reference to the U.S. Navy's Whidbey Island (LSD-41) class amphibious ships, which have a full load displacement of about 15,800 tons.
[227] John J. Tkacik, Jr., *China's Quest for a Superpower Military,* Heritage Foundation Backgrounder No. 2036, May 17, 2007, p. 131.
[228] 2005 RAND report, pp. 147-148.
[229] 2004 ONI WMC, p. 38.
[230] Bill Gertz, "Chinese Hackers Prompt Navy College Site Closure," *Washington Times,* November 30, 2007. Bracketed material as in the original.
[231] John J. Tkacik, Jr., *China's Quest for a Superpower Military,* Heritage Foundation Backgrounder No. 2036, May 17, 2007, p. 17.
[232] *The Chinese Military, An Emerging Maritime Challenge,* Washington, Lexington Institute, 2004, pp. 13-14.
[233] 2005 DOD CMP, p. 40.
[234] A report by the Office of Technology Assessment (a congressional support agency that was closed in 1995), states: "The size of the area that could be affected by EMP is primarily determined by the height of burst and is only very weakly dependent on the yield." (*MX Missile Basing.* Washington, Office of Technology Assessment, 1981. (September 1981) p. 297. The document is available on the Internet at [http://www.wws.princeton.edu/ota/ ns20/year_f.html].
[235] CRS Report RL32544, op cit., states that "creating a HEMP [high-altitude EMP] effect over an area 250 miles in diameter [i.e., a radius of 125 miles], an example size for a battlefield, might only require a rocket with a modest altitude and payload capability that could loft a relatively small nuclear device." One observer states that a detonation height of 200

kilometers (108 nautical miles) would produce an EMP effect out to a radius of about 1,600 kilometers (864 nautical miles), while a detonation height of 50 kilometers would produce an EMP effect out to a radius of about 800 kilometers (432 nautical miles). (Written Statement by Dr. Michael Bernardin, Provost for the Theoretical Institute for Thermonuclear and Nuclear Studies, Applied Theoretical and Computational Physics Division, Los Alamos National Laboratory, before the Military Research and Development Subcommittee of the House Armed Services Committee, October 7, 1999.) A map presented by another observer shows that a detonation height of 100 kilometers (54 nautical miles) would produce an EMP effect out to a radius of about 1,000 kilometers (540 nautical miles). (Statement of Dr. Gary Smith, Director, The Johns Hopkins University Applied Physics Laboratory, before Military Research and Development Subcommittee of the House Armed Services Committee, July 16, 1996.) Another published map states that a detonation height of 30 miles would produce an EMP effect out to a radius of 480 miles. A source note attached to the map attributes it to the above-cited July 16, 1997 testimony of Gary Smith. (See page 3 of Jack Spencer, *America's Vulnerability To A Different Nuclear Threat: An Electromagnetic Pulse.* Washington, Heritage Foundation, 2000. 7 pp. (Backgrounder No. 1372, May 26, 2000) The document is available on the Internet at [http://www.heritage.org/Research/MissileDefense/ bg1372. cf m]).

[236] Even if China does not have the capability to command the early detonation of a warhead on a ballistic missile in flight, it could claim afterward that it did.
[237] 2006 DOD CMP, p. 34.
[238] 2004 ONI WMC, p. 39.
[239] *Fisher 7/27/05 testimony*, p. 6. A footnote at this point in Fisher's statement says this information was: "Disclosed to the author by a U.S. source in September 2004." See also page 9.
[240] Spoken testimony of Richard D. Fisher, Jr., in transcript of *7/27/05 HASC hearing*, in response to a question from Representative Curt Weldon.

Excerpted from CRS Report RL33153, dated June 15, 2007

INDEX

A

access, vii, viii, 23, 29, 30, 31, 32, 36, 37, 40, 43, 74, 76, 94, 95, 99, 114, 119
accounting, 19
accuracy, 22, 71, 72, 120
acoustic, 25, 61, 64, 81, 122
acquisitions, 32, 33, 82
Admiral Michael Mullen, 2, 64
advisory body, 4
Afghanistan, 47, 48, 74
Africa, 49, 73
age, 99, 117
aging, 8, 10
aid, 12, 35
air, vii, viii, 2, 3, 6, 7, 10, 14, 15, 16, 20, 21, 22, 23, 24, 25, 26, 27, 28, 29, 30, 31, 33, 37, 40, 51, 52, 55, 56, 58, 59, 60, 62, 63, 74, 75, 76, 77, 78, 82, 84, 85, 89, 90, 92, 94, 101, 104, 106, 107, 117
Air Force, 3, 7, 23, 24, 27, 28, 37, 48, 58, 59, 75, 77, 80, 84, 93, 98, 107, 117
air-independent propulsion (AIP), 63, 82, 83, 122
airborne warning and control system (AWACS), 7, 20, 86
aircraft, vii, viii, 2, 6, 7, 12, 13, 14, 21, 22, 23, 25, 30, 31, 34, 35, 37, 38, 40, 41, 43, 44, 51, 53, 54, 55, 60, 62, 65, 75, 76, 77, 78, 80, 84, 85, 86, 87, 90, 94, 95, 103, 111, 113, 114, 115, 117
airplanes, 54, 115
Alaska, 79
allies, 50
alternative, 57
ambiguity, 63
American Enterprise Institute (AEI), 42, 48, 114, 115
amphibious ships, vii, 17, 91, 112, 123
analysts, vii, 11, 14, 19, 30, 31, 33, 43, 53, 80
annual rate, 11
anti-access force, vii, 31
anti-air warfare (AAW), vii, viii, 15, 16, 20, 23, 24, 26, 59, 60, 101, 118
anti-satellite (ASAT), 69
anti-ship cruise missiles (ASCMs), vii, 6, 7, 8, 14, 15, 16, 19, 31, 35, 40, 53, 59, 60, 74, 99, 101, 117, 118
anti-ship missiles, 76, 88, 94
antisubmarine warfare (ASW), vii, viii, 13, 20, 21, 22, 25, 35, 41, 42, 52, 54, 61, 62, 63, 64, 78, 80, 106, 109, 111, 113, 114, 115, 121
ants, 29
appendix, 71
application, 95
appraisals, 10
armed forces, 2, 107
Armed Services Committee, 1, 4, 7, 65, 99, 103, 104, 105, 110, 118, 124

Army, 3, 27, 47, 48, 56, 57, 86, 103, 107
ASEAN, 21
Asia, 36, 106
Asian, 22, 33, 73, 75, 78, 109, 111
Assassin's Mace, 72, 96
assault, 87, 91
assessment, 70, 84, 108
assets, 10, 17, 24, 28, 55, 58, 69, 72, 100, 109
Atlantic, 50, 63
atmosphere, 19, 55, 94
atrophy, 41, 63
attacker, 92
attacks, 10, 18, 28, 29, 30, 37, 59, 60, 65, 67, 92, 100, 109
attention, 2, 8, 81
Australia, 17, 113
automation, 23
autonomous, 42, 61, 114
availability, 105
aviation, 24, 27, 49, 84, 86
awareness, 42, 114

B

ballistic missile (s), viii, 3, 5, 6, 8, 10, 11, 19, 27, 30, 55, 56, 57, 71, 72, 73, 74, 79, 96, 98, 109, 119, 120, 121, 124
Bangladesh, 36
barriers, 39
battery, 60, 122
beams, 95
behavior, 32
Beijing, 14, 21, 28, 29, 30, 32, 33, 34, 72, 76, 78, 81, 84, 86, 108, 111, 112, 115, 120
beliefs, 67
benefits, 79, 86
Black Sea, 84
blog, 12, 100, 101
boats, 9, 10, 11, 13, 60, 61, 73, 79, 80, 82, 83, 100
Boeing, 85
Booz Allen, 36
Boston, 108
breakfast, 2, 58
bubbles, 100

buffer, 75
Burma, 36
business, 42
bypass, 37

C

C4ISR, vii, 6, 20, 23, 30, 33, 95
calculus, 42
California, 79
Cambodia, 36
campaigns, 29
candidates, 115
capacity, 6, 30, 57, 75, 79, 87, 88, 89, 92, 122
capital, 84
carbon monoxide, 83
cargo, 77, 86
Caribbean, 49, 50
carrier, 12, 13, 14, 23, 30, 34, 35, 38, 39, 40, 51, 54, 58, 63, 66, 67, 71, 72, 73, 78, 80, 84, 85, 86, 87, 95, 99, 109, 111, 113, 115
cast, 52
cell, 122
certainty, 38
channels, 39, 72
Chief of Naval Operations, 2, 41, 42, 64, 118
Chief of Staff, 111
Chinese, viii, 2, 5, 10, 11, 12, 13, 14, 15, 16, 17, 18, 21, 22, 23, 24, 25, 26, 29, 30, 33, 34, 35, 42, 48, 53, 57, 66, 69, 71, 72, 73, 75, 76, 77, 78, 79, 80, 81, 82, 84, 85, 86, 87, 88, 89, 90, 93, 95, 98, 99, 100, 101, 102, 103, 105, 106, 107, 108, 110, 111, 112, 116, 117, 121, 122, 123
chlorine, 83
civilian, 19, 73, 91, 95
classes, 2, 8, 11, 14, 15, 16, 17, 88, 89, 91, 92, 100, 105
classification, 62
classified, 1, 41, 92
closure, 29
coatings, 10, 85
cocoon, 26
codes, 92
Cold War, 19, 31, 45, 53, 63, 119

Index

Colombia, 63
combat, 1, 2, 7, 16, 21, 24, 26, 27, 40, 58, 59, 75, 85, 91, 99, 107
commerce, 34
commercial, 22, 36, 94, 95, 122
Committee on Intelligence, 7, 99, 103, 105, 110
Committee's Military Commission (CMC), 28
communication (s), vii, 20, 21, 23, 26, 28, 30, 32, 33, 34, 62, 72, 74, 94, 99, 104, 113, 119
community, 121
compatibility, 44
complementary, 53
components, 22, 95, 120
composite, 81
computer (s), vii, viii, 18, 20, 23, 28, 30, 43, 59, 65, 92, 93, 94, 95
computer systems, 18
computer use, 93
confidence, 28, 92, 111, 120
conflict, vii, viii, 3, 18, 19, 29, 30, 31, 32, 33, 36, 37, 38, 40, 43, 44, 48, 51, 52, 59, 60, 65, 92, 103, 109, 112, 119
Congress, vii, viii, 1, 3, 4, 42, 47, 49, 56, 57, 69, 97, 113, 115, 116, 117, 118, 119
Congressional Budget Office (CBO), 51, 115
conjecture, 49
consensus, 80
construction, 9, 10, 11, 15, 16, 26, 27, 34, 51, 77, 79, 82, 84, 87, 89, 91, 105
consumers, 18
contingency, 109
continuing, 24, 31, 84, 86, 107
control, vii, 7, 20, 21, 22, 23, 26, 31, 33, 42, 52, 77, 99, 102, 112, 123
controlled, 16, 17, 102, 111
coordination, 25, 33
Cooperative Engagement Capability (CEC), 59, 117
corruption, 92
cost-effective, 54
costs, 55, 84, 101
countermeasures, vii, 17, 18, 20, 24, 25, 26, 42, 52, 65, 74, 104, 112
coverage, 24, 99

critical assets, 55, 58
CRS, 39, 51, 52, 57, 65, 100, 101, 103, 104, 109, 112, 113, 115, 116, 117, 118, 119, 120, 123, 124
cruciform, 81
crude oil, 122
cruise missiles, 6, 14, 27, 30, 52, 55, 73, 75, 90, 99, 117, 122

D

danger, 96
database, 92
deception, 92
Decision Support System (DSS), 62
decisions, vii, 3, 99
declassified, 11, 12
defense (s), viii, 1, 2, 3, 4, 6, 7, 12, 13, 14, 16, 18, 19, 20, 21, 22, 23, 24, 25, 27, 28, 29, 30, 31, 36, 41, 47, 51, 55, 56, 57, 58, 59, 60, 62, 64, 65, 66, 69, 71, 73, 74, 75, 76, 78, 85, 87, 88, 89, 90, 93, 101, 104, 106, 107, 115, 117, 119, 120
Defense Science Board (DSB), 117
deficiency, 21, 25, 117
degradation, 26, 94
degrading, 22
degree, 65, 88, 94, 105
delays, 55, 106
delivery, 8, 77, 82, 86
demand, 19
denial, 23, 30, 31, 76, 92, 108
Department of Defense (DOD), viii, 3, 4, 5, 6, 7, 12, 13, 14, 15, 16, 17, 18, 20, 23, 25, 28, 29, 30, 31, 32, 33, 39, 40, 47, 48, 55, 57, 58, 72, 74, 75, 76, 79, 80, 91, 93, 94, 95, 97, 98, 99, 101, 102, 103, 104, 105, 106, 107, 108, 109, 110, 111, 113, 115, 117, 119, 120, 121, 123, 124
Department of State, 3
derivatives, 73
desire, 33
destroyers, 2, 6, 14, 15, 16, 23, 24, 25, 26, 33, 38, 40, 44, 50, 53, 54, 55, 57, 60, 82, 84, 85, 87, 89, 90, 101, 105, 109, 115

destruction, 1, 41
detection, 61, 62, 114
deterrence, 50, 107
detonation, 19, 94, 95, 123, 124
diesel, 10, 11, 12, 22, 41, 61, 62, 69, 78, 80, 81, 83, 88, 100, 113, 122
diesel-electric submarine, 12, 69
Director of National Intelligence, 5, 34, 98, 110
discipline, 119
disclosure, 115
displacement, 90, 123
disputes, 32
Distributed Netted Sensors (DNS), 61
division, 50
dominance, 18, 19
Donald Winter, 1
dry, 84
durability, 120
duration, vii, 29, 31, 37, 52, 65
duties, 24, 60

E

early warning, 33
East Asia, 78, 106, 109
eavesdropping, 36
economic, vii, 3, 28, 29, 33
economic assistance, 33
economic policy, 3
economy (ies), 32, 34, 101
education, 20
Education, 19
electrical, 14, 26, 104
electromagnetic, viii, 18, 19, 65, 67, 94, 96, 104, 119
electromagnetic pulse (EMP), viii, 19, 37, 43, 53, 65, 66, 67, 94, 96, 103, 119, 123
electron, 60
electronic (s), 15, 18, 19, 22, 24, 26, 29, 36, 60, 65, 67, 74, 85, 87, 88, 92, 95, 103, 104, 106, 119, 123
electronic circuits, 19
electronic countermeasures (ECM), 26
electronic surveillance, 103

electronic systems, 19, 65, 85
electronic warfare, 18, 29, 92, 106
employment, 86, 119
endurance, 24, 122
energy, vii, 10, 32, 33, 34, 36, 60, 95, 112
engagement, 50, 72, 90
engines, 83, 85, 101, 105, 123
English, 66, 97
enterprise, 117
envelope, 100
environment, viii, 24, 25, 26, 37, 42, 43, 67, 114, 119
environmental, 83
equipment, 21, 22, 26, 27, 33, 41, 49, 63, 87, 91, 101, 104, 120
erosion, 119
estimating, 58
Europe, 50
European, 74
evidence, 18, 22, 93, 94, 112
evolution, 10, 89
evolutionary, 77
exercise, 24, 29, 66, 77
expertise, 18
experts, 74, 80, 81
exploitation, 18
explosive, 66, 95, 96
exports, 99
eye, 107

F

F-16, 58, 77
failure, 108
false, 18, 64
family, 74, 75, 90
Far East, 26
February, 1, 4, 7, 56, 97, 98, 99, 105, 110, 113, 115
Federation of American Scientists (FAS), 11, 12, 100, 101
feet, 22, 104
fighters, 6, 7, 40, 51, 58, 59, 76, 77, 84
finance, 33
financial resources, 57

fire, 26, 29, 77
firms, 106
fishing, 73
fixed targets, 5
flight, 13, 41, 55, 77, 84, 117, 120, 124
floating, 14, 67
forensic, 93
fossil fuel (s), 32
fragmentation, 55
France, 16, 102
Freedom of Information Act (FOIA), 11, 12
friendly nations, 44
fuel cell, 122
funding, 3, 37, 47, 48, 56, 57, 75

G

gas, 32, 35, 88, 100, 101, 105
gauge, 109
General Accounting Office, 114, 117
General Political Department (GPD), 28
generation, 6, 7, 8, 22, 27, 58, 59, 75, 76, 77, 88
generators, 18, 95
Germany, 73
global war on terror (GWOT), 47, 48, 115
goals, vii, 32, 92
government, 12, 13, 14, 26, 35, 84, 99, 108
Government Accountability Office (GAO), 59, 114, 117
grades, 28
graph, 10, 100
ground-based, 58
groups, 27, 30, 33, 35, 36, 47, 63, 71, 73, 78, 80, 89, 95, 119
Guam, 6, 30, 34, 37, 38, 39, 40, 44, 45, 51, 62, 110, 113, 116
guidance, 6, 20, 30, 72
guns, 26

H

hackers, 93
Hainan Island, 37

hardness, 104
Hawaii, 38, 39, 40, 44, 45, 51, 79
hearing, 4, 11, 65, 67, 96, 97, 98, 99, 100, 103, 105, 106, 107, 108, 110, 113, 116, 120, 121, 122, 124
height, 123
helicopters, 41, 42, 54, 87, 91, 92
heme, 14
high-power microwave (HPM), vii, 19, 65, 95, 103, 104
high-speed, 17, 100, 122
high-tech, 21, 27
hip (s), 20, 26, 28, 45, 54, 81, 87, 91, 102
Hong Kong, 85
horizon, 22, 33, 72
hostility, 29
House, 4, 65, 69, 103, 104, 118, 124
hub, 87
human, 115
hunting, 25

I

ice, 7, 99, 105, 110
identification, 114
images, 86
imports, 19, 26, 32, 33, 105, 112
inactive, 12
independence, 32
India, 112
Indian Ocean, 38, 49, 50, 108
indication, 33
indicators, 23, 109
indigenous, 7, 13, 26, 31, 74, 76, 77, 81, 86, 106
industrial, 3, 53, 76, 106
industry, 3, 4, 19, 22, 57, 87, 88, 89, 92, 105, 122
Information Operations, 18, 92
information systems, 18, 27
information technology, 18
infrared, 18
infrastructure, 6, 28, 30, 87, 119
innovation, 89
inspection, 100

inspections, 29
instruments, 21
integration, 21, 22, 26, 76, 105
integrity, 86, 92
intelligence, vii, 20, 23, 36, 52, 86, 92, 115, 119, 121
Intelligence Community, 23, 31, 91
intentions, 14, 20, 69, 86
intercontinental ballistic missile (ICBM), 72
interference, 104
international, 29, 33, 35, 69, 103, 107
Internet, 85, 92, 97, 104, 114, 115, 118, 123, 124
intervention, vii, 29, 30, 32, 34, 96, 107, 108
interview, 93
intrusions, 92, 93
investment, 6, 30, 62, 64
ionization, 94
ionosphere, 94
Iraq, 47, 48, 74, 112
island, 6, 29, 30, 32
isolation, 81
Israel, 65, 66, 67, 73, 74, 99
Italy, 102

J

Jamestown, 110
January, 5, 18, 34, 53, 69, 77, 90, 98, 99, 103, 110, 112, 113, 114, 118, 122, 123
Japan, 6, 12, 13, 30, 33, 35, 37, 38, 40, 44, 45, 87, 94, 108, 110, 111
Japanese, 13, 16, 34, 35, 77, 110, 111
Jefferson, 116
John F. Kennedy, 115
judge, 6

K

knees, 24
knots, 38, 39, 100
Korea, 37, 113

L

LAN, 26
land, vii, 2, 5, 6, 7, 19, 30, 34, 37, 39, 40, 48, 49, 51, 54, 73, 75, 80, 91, 99, 115
land-attack cruise missiles (LACMs), vii, 6, 8, 19, 30, 37, 40, 51, 73, 80
language, 97
large-scale, 21
laser (s), 60, 75, 76, 95, 104
LDP, 92
lead, 19, 33, 48, 72, 80, 111
leadership, vii, 28, 31, 32, 94, 98
learning, 101
legislation, 4
likelihood, 3, 41, 50
limitations, vii, 20, 21, 52, 65, 105
links, 24, 33, 62, 72, 94
literature, 95
Littoral Combat Ship (LCS), 39, 60, 118
localization, 62, 114
location, 6, 30, 38, 73
logistics, vii, 20, 21, 23, 25, 29, 30, 76, 80, 105, 107
long-range surveillance, vii
long-term, 33, 78, 87
Los Angeles, 53, 81, 110, 116
losses, 26
lying, 103

M

machinery, 85
magnetosphere, 94
maintenance, 21, 26, 50, 51, 53, 99, 119
management, 25, 26, 89, 92
maneuverable reentry vehicles (MaRVs), 5, 6, 40, 41, 56, 57, 71, 72
Manhattan, 119
manufacturing, 73
mapping, 92
Marine Corps, 48, 58

Index

maritime, vii, viii, 6, 7, 23, 25, 27, 29, 31, 32, 33, 34, 40, 41, 43, 48, 49, 54, 62, 76, 78, 112, 115
market (s), 32, 85, 90
measures, 18, 30, 43, 104, 115
mechanical, iv, 26
media, 12, 82, 84, 111
Mediterranean, 38, 49, 50
metals, 32
microwave, vii, 19, 65, 95, 104
Middle East, 36, 109, 112
military, vii, viii, 1, 2, 3, 4, 5, 14, 18, 19, 20, 21, 23, 27, 28, 29, 30, 32, 33, 34, 35, 36, 37, 43, 44, 47, 48, 52, 65, 66, 69, 70, 71, 72, 73, 76, 77, 79, 85, 86, 87, 91, 92, 93, 95, 96, 99, 101, 104, 106, 107, 108, 109, 112, 115, 119
mine countermeasures (MCM), vii, 17, 20, 25, 42, 65
mine warfare, viii
mines, vii, 8, 17, 18, 19, 25, 31, 40, 42, 52, 60, 65, 94, 95, 102, 112, 118
mining, 29
Minnesota, 79
missile defense, viii, 55, 56, 57, 58, 72, 109, 119, 120
Missile Defense Agency's (MDA), 55, 56
missile launchers, 72
missiles, 2, 5, 6, 14, 21, 22, 26, 27, 28, 30, 33, 41, 52, 53, 55, 56, 58, 60, 71, 72, 73, 74, 75, 77, 79, 85, 89, 90, 94, 95, 96, 98, 99, 109, 117, 119, 120, 122
missions, 24, 49, 52, 53, 58, 60, 85, 89, 99
mobility, 107
models, 40, 75
modernization, vii, viii, 1, 3, 4, 5, 8, 12, 14, 15, 20, 24, 27, 28, 29, 32, 33, 34, 36, 47, 48, 49, 50, 51, 52, 54, 56, 57, 59, 61, 70, 71, 77, 78, 99, 105, 109, 122
modernize, 15
modules, 22, 77
money, 21, 48
morning, 49
Moscow, 85
movement, 87

N

national, 48, 69, 86, 104, 107, 119
national interests, 86
national security, 48, 69
NATO, 31
natural resources, 32
naval mines, vii, 17, 19, 42
navigation satellites, 74
navigation system, 72, 119
Navy Area Defense (NAD), 55
network, viii, 18, 23, 28, 30, 41, 42, 43, 45, 65, 92, 93, 109, 114
networking, 42, 59, 61
New York, 103, 108, 111
nodes, 52
noise, 81
non-nuclear, 8, 19, 63, 74, 80, 96, 121, 122
Norfolk, 93
novelty, 77
nuclear, vii, viii, 8, 10, 19, 23, 27, 34, 37, 40, 43, 45, 52, 53, 63, 65, 66, 74, 77, 78, 79, 80, 81, 85, 94, 95, 96, 103, 119, 121, 122, 123
nuclear power, 8, 85, 119
nuclear weapons, vii, viii, 37, 43, 65, 66, 94, 103, 119

O

obsolete, 11, 21, 100
oceans, 13
Office of Technology Assessment, 123
offshore, 27, 78
off-the-shelf, 95
Ohio, 81
oil, 32, 36, 112, 122
online, 12, 88, 100, 101, 109
optimism, 2
orbit, 95
organic, 23, 91
organization (s), 25, 28, 53, 98, 119
oversight, 47, 57, 59, 99
over-the-horizon (OTH), 72

P

Pacific, viii, 6, 11, 12, 30, 31, 33, 34, 36, 38, 40, 44, 50, 51, 53, 59, 63, 106, 108, 113, 115, 118
Pakistan, 36, 74, 102
paper, 2, 20, 27, 33, 97, 107
passive, 61, 64, 114
pearls, 36, 117
peers, 119
Pentagon, 12, 66, 79, 93, 94, 96, 97, 108, 109, 112
perception (s), 34, 119
performance, 43, 55, 64, 85, 90, 104
permit, 6, 10, 31, 33, 37, 50, 79, 117, 119
Persian Gulf, 36, 38, 49, 50, 112
Peru, 63
Philippines, 94, 113
photographs, 86
physical environment, 43
pilot training, 13
piracy, 34, 112
planar, 89
planning, viii, 21, 25, 47, 48, 49, 50, 52, 56, 57, 72
platforms, viii, 6, 17, 37, 52, 53, 54, 61, 62, 65, 74, 77, 81, 87, 88, 105, 114, 115
play, 25, 88
pleasure, 112
poisoning, 83
policymakers, 31, 43
political, 3, 19, 28, 29, 37, 44, 74, 76, 84, 98, 108
political leaders, 28, 44
poor, 41, 55, 103
population, 28
ports, 29, 30, 38, 51, 55
posture, 25, 50
power, vii, 4, 19, 23, 34, 36, 37, 65, 72, 78, 80, 94, 95, 104, 105, 106, 108, 112, 117
power plant (s), 105
premium, viii, 37, 44
preparation, 72
pressure, 29
priorities, 27

private, 12, 93
probe, 53
production, 7, 15, 16, 17, 22, 26, 31, 53, 75, 76, 77, 82, 83, 88, 89, 91, 92, 101, 105, 106, 116, 122
professionalism, 22
professionalization, 20
program, 11, 14, 18, 55, 56, 57, 64, 76, 78, 81, 84, 98, 99, 120
proliferation, 90
promote, 107
propagation, 61, 62
propulsion, 10, 15, 22, 63, 78, 82, 83, 87
protection, 119
psychological, 92
public, 19, 95
pulse (s), viii, 19, 65, 67, 94, 95, 96, 119
pumps, 81

Q

Quadrennial Defense Review, 1, 30, 50, 109, 115

R

radar, 2, 16, 26, 28, 55, 56, 57, 59, 60, 67, 71, 72, 74, 85, 89, 90, 94, 117
radiation, 43, 76
radio, 19, 95, 96
radiofrequency, 95
radius, 19, 94, 104, 123
range, 5, 6, 7, 16, 20, 21, 22, 23, 24, 30, 31, 33, 34, 35, 37, 45, 49, 55, 64, 71, 72, 73, 74, 75, 76, 79, 85, 86, 87, 89, 90, 95, 98, 100, 104, 106, 111, 117, 119, 121
reading, 97
real time, 72
realism, 20
reconnaissance, vii, 7, 20, 23, 33, 52, 76, 99
reduction, 51, 81
redundancy, 79
reentry vehicles (RVs), 71
refining, 72

regional, vii, 5, 6, 30, 32, 33, 44, 109, 119
regular, 35
reinforcement, 119
relationships, 36
reliability, 62
repair, 26, 50, 86, 113
Republican, 1
research, 7, 27, 61, 64, 66, 78, 81, 85, 119
Research and Development (R and D), 61, 64, 103, 104, 124
researchers, 53
resistance, 100
resolution, 30
resources, 20, 32, 33, 48, 57, 86
response time, 39
responsibilities, 49
restructuring, 27
retired, 44, 54
Rhode Island, 93
risk (s), 6, 19, 29, 30, 108, 119
rubber, 122
Russia, 8, 9, 10, 14, 18, 74, 75, 76, 77, 81, 82
Russian, 6, 7, 8, 10, 11, 15, 16, 26, 74, 75, 76, 77, 79, 80, 81, 82, 84, 85, 86, 89, 90, 100, 102, 109

S

sabotage, 28
safety, 112
satellite, 72, 73, 74, 75, 115, 119
school, 93
scientists, 81
seabed, 45
searching, 35
Seattle, 113
secret, 84
Secretary of Defense, 70, 97, 117
Secretary of the Navy, 1
security, viii, 22, 33, 34, 36, 43, 48, 65, 69, 84, 93
Self, 13, 35, 111
Self Defense Forces, 111
Senate, 1, 7, 99, 103, 105, 110

sensors, 13, 15, 25, 26, 33, 41, 42, 61, 64, 72, 83, 94, 113, 114
September 11, 111
series, 15, 16, 80, 109
services, 20, 25, 47, 48, 58, 92, 101, 107
shape, 87
shipping, 25, 33, 39, 94, 112
shock, 72, 86, 122
shoot, 53, 55, 75, 82
shores, 86
shortage, 21
short-duration conflict, vii
short-range, 5, 23, 24, 71, 89
short-range ballistic missiles (SRBMs), 5, 56, 71, 98
short-term, 108
sign, 66
signals, 74
silver bullet, 72
simulation, 66, 119
Singapore, 38, 39, 40, 44, 45, 113
sites, 28, 41, 52
skills, 13, 92
skimming, 117
smuggling, 34
society, 119
software, 18, 26
solid state, 60
SONG-class, 69
South Africa, 73
South America, 49, 63, 118
South Korea, 37, 113
Southeast Asia, 33
sovereignty, 112
Soviet Union, 14, 31, 80
specialists, 73
spectrum, 94, 119
speculation, 84
speed, 17, 39, 71, 72, 89, 100, 114, 122
stability, 88, 89
stabilize, 10
stages, 26, 51
standards, 85
strains, 107

strategic, 2, 27, 32, 33, 34, 36, 69, 70, 78, 79, 80, 107, 119
strategies, 4, 29, 36
strength, 10, 107
stress, 49
stretching, 36
strikes, 18, 28, 76, 107
students, 93
submarines, vii, viii, 2, 6, 7, 8, 10, 11, 12, 13, 22, 23, 25, 31, 33, 34, 35, 38, 40, 41, 42, 45, 50, 51, 52, 53, 54, 60, 61, 62, 63, 64, 74, 77, 78, 79, 80, 81, 83, 85, 87, 100, 109, 121, 122
suffering, 26
superiority, 31, 78, 107
suppliers, 21, 22
supply, 18, 21, 25, 33
supply chain, 18, 21
surface-to-air missiles (SAMs), vii, 7, 22, 40, 74, 75, 76, 88, 89
surplus, 95
surprise, 72, 82
surveillance, vii, 6, 10, 20, 23, 24, 41, 43, 45, 52, 54, 72, 103, 115
survivability, 81, 119
surviving, 88
Sweden, 118
systems, vii, viii, 5, 6, 7, 10, 14, 15, 16, 18, 19, 20, 21, 22, 23, 24, 26, 27, 30, 31, 35, 41, 42, 43, 49, 58, 59, 60, 61, 64, 65, 72, 73, 74, 77, 85, 87, 88, 90, 93, 95, 99, 101, 104, 105, 106, 111, 114, 117, 119

T

tactics, 18, 27, 33, 85, 113
Taiwan, vii, viii, 3, 5, 6, 7, 12, 23, 24, 26, 28, 29, 30, 31, 32, 33, 34, 36, 37, 38, 39, 40, 41, 43, 44, 48, 51, 59, 60, 65, 66, 71, 73, 75, 77, 78, 87, 91, 94, 96, 99, 102, 103, 107, 108, 109, 112
Taiwan Strait, viii, 7, 32, 33, 36, 37, 38, 39, 43, 44, 48, 51, 59, 60, 65, 75, 77, 99, 108
tankers, 7, 122
tanks, 91, 92

targeting systems, vii, 119
targets, 5, 6, 26, 29, 30, 49, 60, 64, 76, 79, 95, 104, 117
task force, 4, 21, 34, 66, 67, 98, 103, 105, 108, 109, 110, 111, 114, 117
technical assistance, 79
technician (s), 13, 72, 95
technological, 10, 77, 78, 114
technology, 10, 14, 15, 18, 26, 74, 75, 80, 82, 90, 101, 102, 122
television, 104
term plans, 86
territorial, vii, 32, 34, 35
territory, 32, 66
terrorism, 1, 34, 47, 112
terrorist organization, 119
terrorists, 25
testimony, 11, 100, 101, 102, 106, 108, 109, 110, 113, 120, 121, 122, 123, 124
Thailand, 15, 37, 87
theater-range ballistic missiles (TBMs), vii, 5, 19, 31, 37, 40, 41, 51, 53, 56, 57, 71, 72, 98
theory, 19, 27, 113
thermal, 43
thinking, 32, 48, 51
threat (s), 1, 2, 6, 11, 25, 26, 34, 40, 52, 62, 64, 69, 72, 73, 76, 90, 94, 100, 112, 117, 119
threatened, 69
three-dimensional, 90
threshold, 94
Tiananmen Square, 101
time, 11, 14, 22, 29, 31, 32, 35, 38, 39, 40, 41, 42, 43, 44, 48, 53, 54, 57, 62, 63, 67, 72, 79, 80, 83, 84, 86, 88, 89, 92, 93, 111, 117
Tokyo, 39
total product, 77
totalitarian, 2
tracking, 13, 20, 26, 37, 45, 109, 114, 115
trade, 4
traffic, 29
training, 13, 14, 20, 21, 22, 23, 24, 26, 27, 33, 51, 54, 63, 64, 78, 84, 85, 86, 98
transcript (s), 4, 103, 114, 115, 124
transfer, 51, 85, 86

transformation, 53
transition, 11, 29, 114
transmission, 81
transmits, 41
transport, 91, 92
transportation, 30, 33, 94
travel, 32, 38, 39
trend, 12
trucks, 91
Turkey, 84

U

U.S. military, 1, 18, 19, 32, 37, 65, 66, 112
U.S. Pershing-2, 72
Ukraine, 74, 84, 87
uncertainty, 112
unclassified, 4, 41, 93
underwater vehicles, 42, 114
United Kingdom, 87
United States, 2, 3, 7, 10, 18, 19, 29, 31, 37, 39, 40, 49, 53, 69, 78, 79, 94, 98, 99, 100, 101, 103, 105, 110, 112, 117, 119
Unmanned Aerial Vehicles (UAV)s, 7, 62, 72, 73, 76
urban, 107
users, 93
USS Kitty Hawk, 12, 69

V

vector, 62, 85
vehicles, 5, 6, 41, 42, 61, 62, 71, 72, 73, 91, 95, 114, 117, 120
vein, 24
versatility, 89
vertical launch system (VLS), 16, 89, 90
vessels, 2, 11, 17, 22, 24, 25, 82, 87, 88, 89, 92, 100, 105, 111, 122, 123
Vietnamese, 21
Virginia, 1, 53, 81, 113
virus (es), 18, 92

visual, 100
VLA, 61
vortex, 81
vulnerability, 19, 24, 33, 65, 119

W

Wall Street Journal, 110, 111
war, 13, 27, 29, 30, 47, 50, 66, 69, 93, 94, 112
war on terror, 47, 115
warfare, vii, viii, 10, 13, 15, 16, 17, 18, 20, 21, 22, 23, 30, 31, 41, 42, 47, 53, 59, 61, 64, 65, 73, 78, 80, 82, 88, 93, 103, 106, 107, 111, 115
warheads, 5, 19, 30, 72, 96
Warsaw Pact, 31
Washington, 9, 36, 58, 79, 97, 98, 103, 105, 107, 108, 110, 111, 112, 115, 117, 120, 121, 122, 123, 124
Washington Post, 103, 108, 112
water, 2, 9, 18, 23, 24, 43, 61, 62, 81, 82, 86, 100, 112
waterways, 33
weakness, 22, 73, 89
weapons, vii, viii, 1, 15, 19, 20, 21, 23, 24, 26, 33, 37, 41, 42, 43, 44, 60, 62, 65, 66, 71, 72, 75, 76, 89, 94, 95, 96, 103, 104, 106, 111, 119
weapons of mass destruction, 1
websites, 103
West Africa, 49
winning, 2, 65, 107
winter, 122
wireless, 17
withdrawal, 32
workers, 66, 86
writing, 18, 73

Y

yield, 123